Memories of Tug Valley
A Trip Back in Time

Kyle Lovern

Woodland Press, LLC

Published by
WOODLAND PRESS, LLC
w w w . w o o d l a n d p r e s s . c o m

Copyright © 2012, KYLE LOVERN
FIRST EDITION
ISBN 978-0-9852640-3-1

SAN: 2 5 4 – 9 9 9 9

Introduction

I've always loved nostalgia, Appalachian history, and vintage photo images. Here, I've merged all of these elements to produce a book that is very near and dear to my heart—a book of old photos portraying Tug Valley and its history throughout the years.

Photography. It seems I've always appreciated photography, from the time I was a small youngster. Perhaps my interest was first sparked when my sister, Karen, purchased a Kodak cartridge-type camera and I was fortunate enough to use on occasion. It was also fun watching photos develop instantly from a Polaroid camera my half-brother, Melvin Caudill, once owned. I even enjoyed looking through the collection of family pictures and vacation slides taken by my uncle, Don Davis.

Later, as an adult, I was fortunate enough to become a staff writer, sports editor, and photographer for my hometown newspaper, *Williamson Daily News*. On-the-job training helped me sharpen my own photography skills, as I would take photos of important regional news happenings along the way. Some of the equipment I was lucky enough to use, like a 35 mm Nikon camera, black and white printer, and darkroom equipment, helped me grow in my profession. I also developed an even greater appreciation of how much value images hold, and the nostalgic feelings they evoke, now and forever. Whoever coined the phrase "a picture's worth a thousand words," certainly knew what he or she was talking about. A photograph is both enduring and endearing.

Now about this book. Most of us have a fondness for vintage images because they evoke memories and emotions from yesteryear. They give us a feel for the way our ancestors were raised, and show us visually what the world was like in their lifetime. We can see the clothes they wore, the schools they attended, the sports they played, and the way they lived and worked. We see the companies and businesses that were flourishing at the time the snapshots were taken. We see our ancestors on horseback, or guiding a horse-drawn buckboard, before automobiles were invented. We notice dirt roads before paved streets were constructed, and we see famous landmarks and structures from the past that no longer exist. Through these images, we experience what it was like to live in another era.

Through the years I've collected some of the old photographs you'll find in this volume. Some I have taken myself, and others have been submitted to me by local citizens from their personal photo albums. I was fortunate to find several in the *Williamson Daily News* archives.

As you'll likely notice, in some cases, even though the photos were tattered and worn, we tried to use them due to their historical significance. In other cases, because of extremely poor quality, I wasn't able to use certain submissions because they were not the best reproduction quality. So, if your contribution is not in this book, that is the only reason why.

Regardless, I remain thankful to all who submitted photographs, gave historical information, encouraged me, and helped make this volume possible.

* * *

Inside this book, you'll find the rarest of images from the early 1900s through the 1980s.

After the devastating 1977 flood that ravaged the valley, much of the landscape changed. Homes and buildings were washed away by raging, muddy waters of the Tug Fork River. Therefore, the younger generation may be astounded by the way Williamson and surrounding areas looked prior to the flood.

I grew up in Nolan, a town eight miles north of Williamson, on old route U.S. 52. As a child, it was always a treat to get to "go to town." Our county seat was indeed special.

Historic buildings adorned the streets of Williamson, like the large, wood-framed YMCA hotel and restaurant in the east end, or the ornate Mingo County Courthouse that sat where the current structure is located. Most recall the Williamson Fieldhouse adjacent to Lefty Hamilton Park, which was the site of many great football and baseball games.

The gorgeous Cinderella Theater was a place where many were privileged to go see a movie with a date on Friday night, or catch a double-feature matinee on Saturdays. The town had fantastic eateries .... who could forget the popular Brown Derby, or the once famous Lock, Stock, and Barrel? Many will remember eating a hot dog from the Smokehouse, or enjoying Brunswick's chili. I still think the Walnut Room pizzas were the best I've ever had. My wife, Vicki, recalls how her friend, Rita Cantees, whose family owned the Walnut Room, would make them one of those delicious pizzas almost everyday after school. Vicki will also never forget Strosniders' delicious hot fudge sundaes, or Mickel's freshly made milkshakes served right from the cannister. "Oh those were the days my friend. We thought they'd never end."

Many will recall the retail merchants that lined Second and Third Avenues in Williamson. Perhaps you even recall as a child walking into G. C. Murphys and your mouth would instantly water from the wonderful aroma of fresh roasted peanuts and the site of all the varieties of candy on display. Then you might head upstairs to eye the new toys at Hobbs.

Inside you'll discover numerous structures and landmarks throughout the region that are no longer in existence. For example, many of the old schools are no longer standing.

This area has been fortunate to have had many famous people walk on the soil of our small section of the planet: President John F. Kennedy; Heavyweight Boxing Champion of the World Jack Dempsey; Hall of Fame Baseball Player Stan Musial; WVU and NBA basketball legend Jerry West; and others. They are documented inside this volume.

In spite of the time spent organizing and compiling all the material for this project, I've truly enjoyed traveling back in time. I hope you'll also enjoy your walk through the pictorial history of our region, and gain as much inspiration from and admiration for our ancestors as I did while collecting the images.

Kyle Lovern

Note: Unless otherwise indicated, all photographs and images are from the collection of the author, Kyle Lovern.

I dedicate this book to my three precious granddaughters: Gracie and Gabbie Bevins, and Reese Lovern. They are our future generation, and I hope that this book will give them a deeper understanding of their heritage and therefore themselves. Because, indeed, when we have a sense of where we come from, we can see more clearly of where we want to go.

Foreword

Robert H. "Doc" Foglesong
Four Star General (retired), United States Air Force
Proud Hillbilly from the Tug Valley

For those of us who were born and raised in this unique section of Appalachia, we affectionately refer to as the Tug Valley, Kyle has delivered a gift for us all to enjoy. If you ever visited the "Y" in East End, or helped your neighbors following the '77 flood, or heard our fathers talk about the old Coal Field League and the likes of sports names like Stan "The Man" Musial, you will find this collection of photos a real trip down memory lane.

But there is something more fundamental about this work. One way or another, those of us who lived here formed a bond with the Tug Valley and the challenges, successes, tough times, and happy times it has harbored for us inhabitants.

The people who lived here and shaped our character are the most important element of the Tug Valley story. However, I also believe the geography that surrounds this beautiful valley played a role shaping our souls. The hollows and the hills created an environment where neighbors learned early to depend on each other – better said, where neighbors learned that they could depend on each other.

In these hollows, the title "Hillbilly" was not considered a negative, but was a descriptor of a proud tribe of like minded, hard working, honest people who would fight to keep their honor – and their moonshine.

Hillbillies worked in mines, and on the railroad. They were our teachers and our carpenters. They played sports like there was no tomorrow. They went to church to pray for a better tomorrow. Those Hillbillies showed us how to live – some of them showed us how to die in the wars this nation fought. I can tell you from personal experience, you were really happy to have a Hillbilly in your unit or your foxhole.

In a sense, I blame the Tug Valley – its people and its geography – for producing this incredible tribe of resourceful, courageous ridge runners.

What Kyle has done is remind us where we come from – and what we have been about. This collection of photos and memories is great material for all of us Hillbillies who haunted and are haunted by the Tug Valley.

Table Of Contents

A Brief History   Page 9

Old Schools   Page 10

Williamson: The Early Years   Page 18

Tug Valley Sports   Page 43

Flooding In Tug Valley   Page 80

Memories of Nolan   Page 96

Town of Matewan   Page 106

Other Great Communities   Page 118

Railways, Coal, and Timber   Page 131

Memories of Tug Valley   Page 143

Politicians, Civic Leaders & Dignitaries   Page 162

A Brief History

Mingo County is the youngest county in the Great State of West Virginia. It was carved and split from Logan County in 1895.

The county is named in honor of the Mingo Tribe of Native American Indians, which were some of the earliest known inhabitants of the region.

The Tug Fork River, a tributary of the Big Sandy River, snakes through the Tug Valley, dividing West Virginia and Kentucky.

This part of the Appalachian Mountains has a rich history which includes such events as the Hatfield and McCoy Feud and the Glen Alum Train Robbery.

The Town of Matewan was the location of one of the biggest gunfights in U.S. history, the Matewan Massacre. Striking miners, backed by Matewan Police Chief Sid Hatfield, had a violent gun battle with agents from the Baldwin Felts Detective Agency, hired by a coal company to evict coal mining families from company owned "coal camp" houses.

There are five incorporated cities, or towns, in Mingo County: Williamson, Kermit, Matewan, Delbarton, and Gilbert. Many other small communities are spaced in between the narrow valleys and hollows of the county's rough terrain.

Williamson was incorporated in 1892, named in honor of Wallace J. Williamson, the owner of the land where Williamson is now located.

Williamson grew rapidly when the railroad connected into the city to outside areas. Coal and timber industries brought jobs to the area. Soon, Williamson became known as "The Heart of the Billion Dollar Coalfields."

Williamson's population rose from 668 in 1900, to nearly 10,000 by 1930. That population held steady through the war years of the 1940s and 1950s.

Kermit was first known as Lower Burning Creek and East Warfield. (Warfield, KY, is just across the border from Kermit.) The name was changed to Kermit reportedly when a post office was established in 1906. Kermit was named for Kermit Roosevelt, son of President Theodore Roosevelt, and incorporated in 1909.

Today, the entire region continues to grow and modernize, and its industry continues to diversify. Mingo County, in the cradle of the Appalachian Mountain range, is a beautiful region inhabited by proud, hard-working people— *and its best years wait on the horizon.*

Old Schools

Most all of the high schools and grade schools in the area no longer exist, gobbled up by consolidation and closed because of population loss and age. Many of our best memories are from those scholastic days. From the age of about five years old, to graduation day when most of us were either seventeen or eighteen, those school years make up a great amount of our childhood and teenage days. I hope the pictures of these schools bring back many cherished memories.

Williamson High School, which sat along Alderson Street, has many great memories for Wolfpack graduates. The building was used as the junior high school after the newer high school was built and opened in 1974. Eventually those students were moved into the current building and the old brick structure was torn down in the mid 1980s. Williamson High School was formed in 1910 and closed for the current consolidation in 2011. WHS lasted for 101 years, but for those who walked those halls, it will last forever.

Nolan Grade School was located down the street of what many referred to in our community as the "Backway." The Tug River was on one side and the railroad tracks just a few yards away on the other side. The brick structure was the first to be built. Later the front cinder block addition was added. The first school was an old wood-framed house a few yards down the "Backway" from this school. Nolan was consolidated with Riverside in the early 1990s and was bought by the U.S. Army Corp of Engineers for the flood project and torn down.

This image is of the old school building at Chattaroy. It housed both the grade school and the high school, until CHS was consolidated with Williamson in 1962. It became a junior high and grade school, then later just a grade school when CJHS was consolidated with Williamson Junior High in 1984. Later the grade school was also consolidated and joined West End and Nolan to form Riverside in 1993. The brick school was eventually torn down and is now the site of the Chattaroy Volunteer Fire Department. The old gymnasium, which was built in 1940, was used for many years, but eventually was also demolished. Many great memories were made on that old basketball court. The first school at Chattaroy was a 2-story wood frame building. The brick structure pictured here was opened in 1921.

This is the Borderland Grade School, circa 1920. This was one of the many one-room schoolhouses located in the region at the time. (Photo courtesy of Ray Elkins)

West End Grade School sat on West Fifth Avenue just below Slater Street in West Williamson.. Many students went through those narrow hallways. The structure was torn down in the 1990s.

East End Grade, a small community school, sat on the corner of Peter Street and Culross Street. Like most community grade schools, the faculty members taught many youngsters the basics: reading, writing and arithmetic. (Photo courtesy of William Altice)

The Main Building Grade School was located near where the current Williamson Middle School was built. Students from the main and downtown sections of Williamson attended this school. (Photo courtesy of William Altice)

At left, Cinderella Grade School was typical of the coal camp schools that were a part of many hollow or rural communities in Mingo County, especially in the 1930s through the 1950s. This building, first built in 1934, still stands and is part of the Mingo County Board of Education complex on Sycamore Road, or, as it is commonly known, Cinderella Hollow.

Kermit High School was established in 1917. The newer brick high school was built in the 1930s. This photo is believed to be around 1938. The school was eventually consolidated with Lenore to form Tug Valley in the late 1980s. Kermit was known for its success on the hardwood. The school won two state titles, one in 1964 and the other in 1975. The Blue Devils were state runners-up in the old Class B division in 1950. The site of the current Kermit Town Hall is where the old school was located, beside the gymnasium. The gym is still there, the site of many great basketball games over the years. (Courtesy of Kermit Library)

Kermit Grade School is pictured here, before it was demolished for the U. S. Army Corps of Engineers Tug Fork Flood Protection Project. (Courtesy of George and Bobbie Marcum)

In this tattered image, Lenore High School is shown around 1932, as indicated by the vintage automobiles parked at the bottom of the hill. The "new" gymnasium was built and added to the facility around 1970. It was located to the right of the school. The gym still stands, but the school was eventually sold and torn down. (Photo courtesy of Ann Damron)

This image, at left, is of the wood-framed, two-story Lenore Grade School, circa 1912. (Courtesy of Charlotte Sanders)

Here is a photo of the Burch High School building. It was a wood-framed structure that was located on the hillside above the town of Delbarton. Later, a brick and mortar building was constructed. (Photo courtesy of Bert Staton)

Matewan High School building is depicted in this image. This winter scene shows students leaving the school while the snow falls. The school, which featured large white columns in the front of the structure, was flooded several times over the years as the Tug overflowed its banks. (Photo courtesy of Yvonne DeHart)

Red Jacket Junior High School, with adjacent gym, was home to the Indians. The school was consolidated with nearby Matewan, but for years Red Jacket fielded some great football and basketball squads.

In this worn and torn image, taken around 1920, the students are shown at the Narrows Branch one-room grade school near Hardy, KY.

Liberty High School, located just off of Vinson Street in Williamson, was where African-American children and teenagers attended during the days of segregation.

Sprigg Grade School, along Route. 49, this building still stands and was later used by a local coal company.

Taylor School, erected in 1929 and located on the upper end of Martin Co., KY, was a one-room schoolhouse that was built on an 80-foot square parcel of land purchased from John Greene Taylor, who agreed to the sale in order for his grandson to be able to receive his schooling closer to home. Before this, children walked to school at Whitepost, (Big Creek) KY. There were outhouses and a hand-dug well in front. It contained grades 1 through 8. John G. Taylor also bought and donated the school house bell. It remained standing

through the 1977 Flood, and until the construction of Corridor G bought out the property. (Courtesy of Donna Taylor Goble)

Williamson: The Early Years

Williamson, the county seat of Mingo, was incorporated in 1892. Historians say that Williamson was named in honor of Wallace J. Williamson, one of the early settlers of the valley. Much of the region, including portions of Southern West Virginia and Eastern Kentucky, centered around downtown Williamson. The city evolved over the years and became the "Heart of the Billion Dollar Coalfields."

The Norfolk and Western Railroad (now Norfolk Southern) had one of its biggest railroad yards located in the East End of town, including a unique roundhouse.

Buildings that many remember, but no longer exist, include the majestic courthouse, which was torn down in the mid-1960s, and the YMCA building, once believed to be one of the largest wood-frame buildings in the United States.

Many of Williamson's first streets were made of red brick. Some of these streets still exist and have not been paved over. Downtown Williamson thrived with retail stores and locally-owned restaurants.

Some of the photos are from the early 20th Century and date back to the early-1900s.

Above, this vintage post card of downtown Williamson shows the business district, Second Avenue, in the early-1920s. Below, this image of Williamson's Fourth Avenue is believed to have been taken in the 1930s or early-1940s. (Photos courtesy of Eric Simon)

At left, the original City Hall building and fire station that was originally located along Harvey Street and Third Avenue. At right, this snapshot of the Coal House was taken in the early-1930s.

Mr. and Mrs. George Cantees are shown in this old image in the Cantees Confectionary store in Williamson in the mid-1920s. The Cantees family had several thriving businesses in the city over the years, including a department store, the Coca-Cola bottling plant, Walnut Room, Seetnac, Smokehouse, and other restaurants. (Photo courtesy of Jeanette Cantees McCoy)

This image of downtown Williamson's Second Avenue was taken from a tattered postcard, circa 1935. .(Photo courtesy of Eric Simon)

The Easter Arms Hotel. (Photo courtesy of Eric Simon)

This worn photograph depicts the Williamson Railroad Depot, which was a hub of activity within the business district.

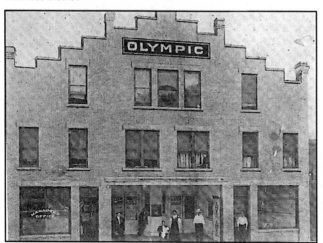

The Olympic building, with its unusual design, was an original three-story downtown fixture within the City of Williamson. The first floor housed several businesses and apartments could be found on the upper floors.

Playing the most popular movies of its day for many years, the Mingo Theater in downtown Williamson was a favorite entertainment center for many Mingo County citizens. (Courtesy of Ed Goff)

The YMCA facility, located at East End, was a hotel and restaurant and was used by many of the railroaders who worked in Williamson and traveled back and forth along the rail line to Bluefield. Above, here is a photo of the "Y" around the time it was first built. Below, here is another view of the massive wood structure.

The historic Cinderella Theater building. Youth, from throughout the area, watched matinees on Saturday afternoon, or popular feature films on Friday nights, at this popular Williamson movie house. Many great movies were shown over the years at this unique theater. Notice the beautifully lighted marquee that jutted out over the sidewalk.

With its massive post-Civil War design, the Mingo County Courthouse, which was located on Second Avenue in downtown Williamson, was a grand structure that was once considered the "heart of the city." In the image you can see the clock tower and the Indian fountain, which was later rebuilt in front of the Coal House.

At left, Strosnider Drug Store on Second Avenue was a thriving local business for decades. At right, for many years, the Tug River Grocery Wholesale building was a well-known business in Williamson.

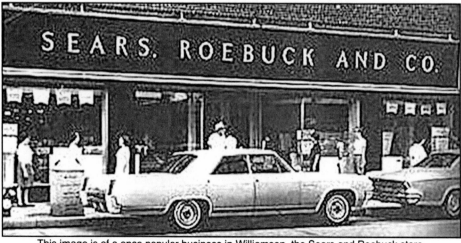

This image is of a once popular business in Williamson, the Sears and Roebuck store.

The Leroy Dairy in Williamson once had a steady business, with hundreds of customers on their route in Mingo County. In the early days, milk and other products were delivered door-to-door by truck drivers. Below, this is the Leroy Dairy headquarters, circa 1930s. In years past, the Williamson area also had the Leatherwood Dairy and Borden's Dairy. In the 1960s, Leatherwood had a huge advertising clock on the hillside overlooking downtown Williamson.

This image is of the C & M Market in the early days of the county seat. (Photos courtesy of William Altice)

The Williamson Fruit Market and Logan Street Grocery in downtown Williamson were hubs of activity in the 1920s through the 1940s. In this image is Daisy Mosley and her daughter, Audrey Mosley. The grocery businesses offered wholesale and retail services and a variety of products, including fresh vegetables, fruits, meats, and general store items. At one time Williamson had several local grocery stores within the business district. (Photo Courtesy of Larry Torlone)

The old National Bank of Commerce Building, located in the center of downtown Williamson.

These two rare post cards were described as birds eye views of Williamson, taken from the hillside above town. (Photo courtesy of Eric Simon)

Joe Mosley operated a quaint grocery on Logan Street, near Williamson High and the Fruit Market. "In the first photo, at left, my grandfather, Joe Mosley, owner of Williamson Fruit Market, stands with employee, Herman Wisecup, in the 1930s. It was located on Third Avenue between Cantees Department Store and Pike Street. The third picture was taken at Logan Street Grocery in the 1950s, which is the store that people from our generation remember. In it are Frank Cricelli, my grandfather's brother, Joe Mosley, holding my brother, Daniel Torlone, and Audrey Mosley. In the last photo Audrey Mosley is holding Daniel Torlone, my mother Daisy Torlone and uncle Frank Cricelli," said Larry Torlone. (Courtesy of Larry Torlone)

This image of the Flowers Bakery building was taken in the late-1950s or early-1960s.

This photograph is of the Norfolk and Western Roundhouse. The roundhouse is still in use today, and is a popular site among railroad enthusiasts.

The First National Bank Building was located at the corner of Second Avenue and Logan Street, and was destroyed by a natural gas explosion years after this image was taken. The banking institution was replaced with its current building.

The South Williamson Bank was located on the Kentucky side of the Tug River. This photograph was taken from a vintage post card.

The Williamson Memorial Hospital was founded in 1918. This building still stands and is used as physicians' offices. The newer hospital at the top of Alderson Street opened in the 1980s. This hospital locally was known as "the hospital on the hill." R. W. Salton and his son, Dr. Russell Salton, ran the hospital for many years. Here, below, are photos of R. W. Salton and George Conley. The hospital also had a nursing school in the facility adjacent to the hospital. The image of the nurse, below, which was contributed by Robin Croaff, shows Virginia Croaff Hall sitting outside the nurse's dorm, circa 1945. She, like many others, attended the local nursing school.

Virginia Croaff Hall

George Conley

R. W. Salton

Appalachian Regional Hospital was built in the late 1950s. It was later refurbished in the early 1990s. Here is an image of the original building. It was built and first operated by the United Mine Workers of America. This hospital was known locally as the "hospital across the river," and was referred to by many as "Miner's Hospital." Some of the older generation still call it that today.

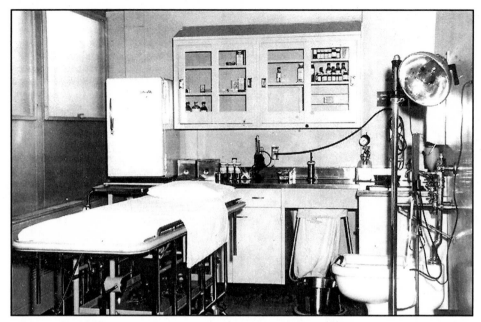

The images on this page were taken when Appalachian Regional Hospital first opened its doors in 1956. One shows a clerical worker at her typewriter, while another shows a pharmacist, with the refrigerator and storage room for pharmaceuticals. Another photo seems to be the administrator and a nurse with a classic sign advertising a blood donor drive. The other photos are of the emergency room, above, and exam room.

In 1956, the United Mine Workers of America (UMWA) and thousands of citizens in the coal communities dedicated the Miners Memorial Hospital Association's (MMHA) facilities. The system's hospitals were located in Harlan, Hazard, McDowell, Middlesboro, Whitesburg, Pikeville and South Williamson, Kentucky; Man and Beckley, West Virginia; and Wise, Virginia. By the early 1960s, MMHA announced its intention to close some of the hospitals and soon after the Board of National Missions formed a new and independent not-for-profit health system Appalachian Regional Hospitals (ARH)--that purchased the Miners Memorial Hospitals. The health system changed its name in 1986 to Appalachian Regional Healthcare to more accurately describe its far-ranging activities.

Bargain Day Parade in downtown Williamson. Old business signs in the background include Esso, Sears and Roebuck, and others. Pictured in this photo are Claude Stowers, P. Dempsey, Josephine Spaulding, Saul Brown and Opal Crum. (Photos courtesy of Jan Webb)

The above two photos were taken during the dedication of the Harvey Street Bridge. (Photos courtesy of Jan Webb)

The Justice Drive Inn was located on the Kentucky side of the Tug River at the end of the Second Avenue Bridge. It was a popular hangout for teens and families. The restaurant was known for its "Chicken in the Box."

This is a photograph of Price Motor Company when it was on Fourth Avenue. The company later moved to Fairview Addition. The Price family ran this new and used car business for many years. (Photo courtesy of William Altice)

Little Venice Pizza was a popular spot for the teenagers in the 1970s and up until the 1990s. It was located near the Sacred Heart Catholic Church on Fourth Avenue.

The old West End swimming pool was destroyed by the 1977 flood, and a newer pool was built afterwards. This pool still exists and provides many residents with hours of summer enjoyment. (Photo courtesy of William Altice)

This image is of the Williamson City Police department from the 1960s, taken in front of the National Guard Armory in West End. Shown are Ernest Deskins, Baa Jordan, Virgil Johnson, Council Adams, Taff Smith, Rossi Bucci, Mooch Justice, Bob Howard, Howard Hatfield, Jolly Smith, Allen "Dopie" Hall and Jimmy Corea. (Photo courtesy of Jolly Smith)

This image is of the Williamson City Police from 1955. From left, Chief Glenn Thompson, George Jackson, Garnet Richmond, Reaford Deskins, Dennis Dudley, Howard Richardson, Rossi Bucci, and Albert "Baa" Jordan are shown. This picture was taken at the old football stadium on the hill during an FBI Training School. (Photo courtesy of the WPD and Chief Dave Rockel.)

This photo shows the Williamson City Police department of 1960. Pictured, front row, left to right, Virgil Johnson, Allen Hall, Albert "Baa" Jordan, Ernest Deskins and Jimmy Corea. Back row, Taff Smith, Bob Howard, Mooch Justice, Howard Hatfield, W.C. "Jolly" Smith, and Council Adams. The picture was taken at the National Guard Armory in West End. (Photo courtesy of the WPD and Chief Dave Rockel)

This photo from the late-1930s is of the Williamson City Police. The image was taken in front of city hall on Harvey Street. (Photo courtesy of Chief Dave Rockel)

This rare photograph depicts the Williamson City Police department from the mid-1940s. Front row, from left, Pierce Maynard, H.H. Davis, Andy Johnson and Tom Maynard. Back row, B.H. Correll, Joe Hunt, Claude Maynard, Bartram, Bill Oney and unknown. (Photo courtesy of Charlotte Sanders)

This image is of Williamson Fire Chief Donald Anderson, taken around 1950. (Photo courtesy of the WFD)

This photo includes members of the Williamson City Police from the mid-1950s. Front row, left to right, Rossi Bucci, Mayor Henry Hammond, Chief Clyde McCoy and Garnett Richmond. Back row, Charlie Hurn, Harold Ford, Thomas "Boxhead" Jones, Jimmy Corea, Tom Maynard, Baa Jordan, W.C. "Jolly" Smith, Reaford Deskins and Ernest Deskins, a merchant policeman. (Photo courtesy of Jolly Smith)

This is the 1974 installment of the Williamson Fire Department (WFD). Several of the photos are displayed at the Grover C. "Curt" Phillips Emergency Services Building, which now houses the fire and police departments for the city. Other photos are also on the department's website. Front row, left to right, Emery Mounts, Ralph Hill, Butch Beckett, Gary Corea and Jerry Mounts. Back row, Curt Phillips, Delaney Stowers, Bobby Ryan, Charlie Smith, Paul Phillips, Bryan Jude and Henry McKnight. (Photos courtesy of WFD Chief Jerry Mounts)

At left, this image is of the Williamson Fire Department firefighters from 1944. At right, the photograph is of the Williamson Fire Department members from 1950. Below, in this 1950 photo, the WFD displays their iron lungs, which were utilized to transport tuberculosis patients. At the time, the only emergency ambulance service in the area was the Williamson Life Saving Crew. (Photos courtesy of the WFD)

This photo of downtown Williamson at night was used as a postcard in the 1970s. Red strobe lights could be seen from the radio tower that sat atop the Mountaineer Hotel, later moved to the mountaintop above East End when WBTH, a longtime AM radio station, was joined by WXCC, a new FM station in the early 1980s.

This photograph depicts street construction teams on the job in the City of Williamson. The early streets were first paved with bricks, and preparation was done by hand. Rock and other material was moved from the location by horse and mule teams and wagons.

Above, the Mountaineer Hotel, located in downtown Williamson, housed several celebrities over the years, including presidential candidate John F. Kennedy in 1960. Entertainers and sports celebrities also stayed at the historic hotel through the years, including Jack Dempsey, Stan Musial, Loretta Lynn, Tex Ritter, and others. At right top, and below, construction on Williamson's infamous hairpin curve was originally dug by hand. The "Hairpin" connects Vinson Street with East Fourth Avenue, which is a part of U.S. 52 that travels south to East End and on to Cinderella Hollow.

The old Second Avenue Bridge, a steel structure that stood in Williamson for decades, was eventually replaced with a modern structure. Many in Mingo County fondly recall this old bridge. (Photo courtesy of William Altice)

The Wells Goodykoontz home in Williamson, with its classic design, white columns, and elegant masonry work, was very "well to do" for its generation. This photograph, used as a postcard, was taken in the 1920s.

Once a landmark in the community, the Williamson Presbyterian Church was a popular house of worship within the city limits. This photo was taken in early-1920s.

This vintage photograph of downtown Williamson was taken around 1918. The city was an extremely busy place at the time and the hub of activity for the county. This snapshot was taken at Second Avenue.

This winter photograph shows city children having fun, sledding down Fourth Avenue Hill. The image was taken in the 1920s.

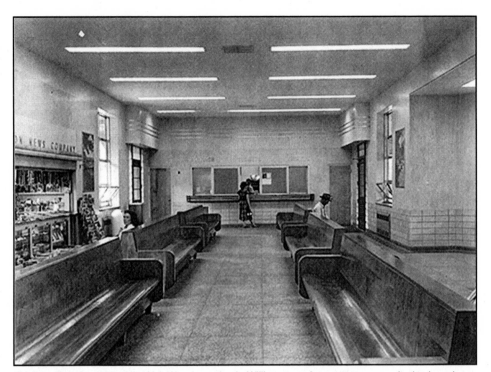

This is an interior view of the N & W train station in Williamson, where customers waited to board passenger trains. In the past, trains were an especially popular and affordable way to travel, and area residents could board a train car in Williamson and travel to places north like Cincinnati, Columbus, or south to Bluefield and beyond.

This image was taken at the Williamson High School swimming pool, located near the "crackerbox" gym. Many hours were spent during the summer months by teens and youngsters swimming and socializing at the pool.

This early photo is of the Logan Street underpass that stretched beneath the railroad tracks and provided a safe pathway for pedestrians.

This image, although worn, shows a section of the City of Williamson, taken during the early-1930s. It was taken of Third Avenue looking westward.

Here is an early photograph of the Williamson Fire Department. The City of Williamson has the only paid firefighters in the county, but also utilizes well-trained, part-time volunteers who make up a large part of the team of firefighters. (Photo courtesy of the WFD)

This rare photograph shows the YMCA facility as it was being built. The multi-story facility, a huge undertaking for its day, eventually served railroad workers, local citizens, and travelers to the area for many years. When completed it offered customers a restaurant, sleep rooms and shelter, and meeting rooms.

This image of Third Avenue in downtown Williamson was taken around 1950. Midge Wolfe is shown walking in front of Cohen Drug. In the background is the Cinderella Theater marquee and the sign for the once popular Starlight Cafe. (Photo courtesy of Charlotte Sanders)

A favorite restaurant, the Lock, Stock and Barrel was located on Second Avenue in Williamson. This popular eatery was a thriving business from the 1960s through the 1980s. Jim Webb, an English instructor at the local community college, is shown sitting on the bench in front of "The Barrel." (Photo courtesy of Glen Simpson)

The community "five and dime," the G. C. Murphy Department Store, on Second Avenue in Williamson was a modern day general store for shoppers in Mingo County. The store sold a variety of items and products, including clothing, shoes, gift items, novelties, and household goods. It also had a fresh candy and peanut counter that was a favorite among area children. The store also sold goldfish and related supplies, and had a complete toy section.

Tug Valley Sports Teams

Sports are one of the primary things that truly bond small communities. Throughout the years many of the high schools in our area have played in state championships. Some of these are among our dearest memories. Many of these squads are on the next few pages, along with some other old photos of youth league teams.

This is the Nolan Midget League Basketball team in 1953: league champs, pictured from left to right, front row, Roy Spradlin and Bobby Smith. Back row, Melvin Caudill, Hubert Jarrell, Lawrence Thompson, Monus Smith and Jimmy Kirk.

This is the Nolan Midget League Basketball team in 1969: the Hornets, front row, left to right, Kyle Lovern, Gary Dove, Jeff Chapman and Glen Roy Smith. Back row, Jimmy Elkins, Greg White, Burnam Davis, Jerome Marcum and Principal and head coach Shayde Chapman.

In this worn image, the 1968 Nolan Midget League team included, front row, left to right, Darrell Spradlin, Jeff Chapman, Luther Montgomery, Jerome Marcum, Hobie Fugett and Max Stroud. Back row, left to right, coach Wallace "Wally" Marcum, Glen Roy Smith, Andrew Marcum, Glen Blevins, Greg White, Burnam Davis and Kyle Lovern.

The championship Chattaroy Midget League team from 1976. Some of those identified in the picture are front row, left to right Melvin Martin, James Teeters, Mike McCoy, Troy Chaffin, Bobby Fletcher and Berman Jewell. Middle row, l to r, Eric Campbell, Billy Preece, Jamie Staten, Rusty Barker, Rob Harris, John Teeters. Back row, L to R: Jeff McCoy, Daryl Evans, Michael Hunter, Kenny Schwartz, Harry Mikailian, Frankie Smith, James Price, Mont Smith. (Photo courtesy of Rob Harris)

This is the Chattaroy Junior High team from 1963. Pictured back row, left to right, student managers Danny Thompson and Perry Cook, Rufus Diamond, Roger Mann, Hawk Chandler, Coach Bob Meade, Lon Steele, Curt Fletcher, Buster White and Garland Kirk, who presented the championship trophy to the Yellowjackets. Front row, Noah "Nopie" Copley, Roger Fletcher, James Atwood, Ronnie Daughtery, Jim Henson and Cody Goodman. (Photo courtesy of Ed Goff)

The Chattaroy Midget League basketball team from the early 1960s. Pictured, front row, left to right, Eugene Hatfield, Tom Fletcher, Roger Fletcher, Johnny Johnson and Ralph Caudill. Back row, coach Joe Spano, Noah "Nopie" Copley, Danny Thompson, James Atwood, Rufus Diamond and coach Ed Goff.

The Chattaroy Junior High girls championship team from 1977. Pictured, front row, left to right, Sharon Davis, Linda Kay Runyon, Lisa Watson, Pam Hensley and Jackie Teeters. Middle row, Loraine Marcum, Linda Barker, Tammy Dillon, Coochie Sorrell, Rhoda Smith, Alvena Allen and Pam Sword. The trophy was presented by Board of Education member Shayde Chapman. Back row, coach Curt Fletcher and BOE member Larry Hamrick. Also in the back were Sherry Fields and Bowens. (Photo courtesy of Rhoda Smith)

A Williamson Midget League football team from the early-1960s. Several of these players went on to play high school and college ball. Among them are Mike Slater who played at WVU and John Yost who played at WV Tech, and many other fine athletes who played for the Williamson Wolfpack. Others in the photo include Steve Tygart, Mike McBrayer, Jerry "Ha-Ha" Davis, Jeff Zappin, Randy Gillispee, Sonny Burmister, Doug Wilburn, Steve Mickey and coaches Elbert Mickey and Jim Reid. (Photo courtesy of Jerry Davis.)

The Chattaroy Junior High basketball team from 1976 went undefeated and won the Mingo County championship. The squad was coached by Curt Fletcher, who later went on to coach at Williamson High School. Pictured, left to right, front row, Kenny Schwartz, Bobby Fletcher, Jimmy Barker, Kenny Jude, Okey Smith, Paul McCoy and Mark Curry. Back row, David Lee Maynard, Fletcher, Chuck Harrison, Dennis Jackson, Pete Smith, Barry Kohari, Brian Coburn, Chuck Alley and Steve White. (Photo courtesy of Okey Smith)

Here is the Town Midget League football team and cheerleaders from the mid 1960s. At that time the local midget league football and basketball teams came from individual schools. Town was the Main Building Grade School in Williamson. Throughout the years there were teams from East End, West End, Chattaroy, South Williamson and Nolan. Individuals in this photo include: front row, left to right, Susan Sherman, Krista Cather, Carla Evans, Anita Brown, Susan Hubbard, Gina Quattro, Gina Martin, Leada Dotson and Debbie Sayers. Second row, Dee Gentile, Joe Hatfield, Tommy Ward, Billy Moses, Mac Hall, John Hagaman, Barry Smith and Larry Smith. Third row, Ronnie Webster, Bobby Casebolt, Hokie Moore, Dawna Taylor, Butch Gregory, Timmy Adams and Joey Jones. Back row, Bobby Phillips, Mark Farmer, Al Plymale, Stephen Younger, Jimmy Hays, Burkie Taylor, Greg Stallard, Joey Jones and Billy Pinson. (Photo courtesy of Al Plymale)

This is the West End Midget League Basketball team in 1969: Some of the players on that squad, in no particular order were Brother Reid, Mickey McKnight, Mark Mitchell, Jeff Jackson, Frank DeMartino, Ted Keith, David Price. The team was coached by Bobby Beckett and Wallace Jewell. (Photo courtesy of Mickey McKnight)

47

The East End Midget League Basketball team 1968, back row, left to right, coach Butch Beckett, Jeb Blevins, Ralph Adkins, Chuck Smith, Danny Kidd, Joe Tincher and assistant coach Ronnie Wingo. Front row, Freddie Ball, Brian Corea, Tony Ramella, Mike Murphy, Mike Neal and Mike Mosko. (Photo courtesy of Mike Murphy)

The 1969 East End team included front row, left to right, Brian Corea, John Davis, Mike Blackwell, Darren Porter, Albert Hairston and unknown. Back row, coach Butch Beckett, Mike Clayborn, Henry Blackwell, Mike Murphy, Jeb Blevins, J. C. Urps, Kenny Porter, Mike Neal and Jim Leftwich. (Photo courtesy of Mike Murphy)

The West End Midget League basketball team from 1968. Some of those identified in the picture in no particular order were Mark Bono, Brother Reid, Mickey McKnight, Rudy Slater, Frank DeMartino, Steve Wilson, Seth Staker, Ronnie Hughes, Ted Keith, David Price, Jeff Jackson and Jon Hess. The coaches were Wallace Jewell and Bobby Beckett. (Photo courtesy of Mickey McKnight)

This is the West End Cheerleader Squad from 1966. Front row, Angela Wellman and Penny Keith. Back row, Elaine Scott, Sue Ellen Sexton, Rebecca Ratliff and Karen Johnson. (Photo courtesy of Angela Wellman)

South Williamson Panthers 1976 - 1st row: Tom Taylor, Bruce Johnson, Bobby Hubbard; 2nd row: Brian Johnson, Mark Cline, Mark Johnson, Ricky West, Gary Smith, Billy Copley; 3rd row: Robin Johnson, Tommy Smith, Matthew Gilliam, Brent Jude, Jerry Darbyshire, James Justice, Dana Tuffland and Coach Paul Thomas.

1975 South Williamson Midget League Champs - sitting Scott Hatfield, Front row: Jeff Tussey, Jerry Darbyshire, Tom Taylor, Mike Sammons, Chris Hatfield, Tim Taylor, Grover Bevins, Dennis Sesco, Greg Hatfield. Back row: Coach Tussey, Eddie Tussey, Matthew Gilliam, Brent Jude, Robin Johnson, Gary Smith, Ricky West and Coach Howard Hatfield.

1976 Panther Basketball - Back row: Matthew "Killer" Gilliam, Gary "The Kid" Smith, Dana Tuffland, Coach Thomas, James Justice, Brent Jude, Jerry "Darb" Darbyshire Tom Taylor; Front Row: Bobby Hubbard, Tommy Smith, Ricky West, Bryan Johnson, Mark Cline, Mark Johnson, unknown, Tim Taylor, and up front, Bruce Johnson.

The 1970-71 South Williamson Grade School team that won the county championship. Pictured, front row, left to right, Barsha Kirk, Tammy Blackburn Murphy, Rhonda Meade Harmon, Alisa Lambert, Cindy Hankins Robertson, Kim Lambert and Kim Hutchins. Middle row, Donnie Goins, Bruce Rosen, Eugene Sesco, Tommy Gilliam, Blair Hampton, Brian Reed, Jeff Jewell, Coach Bill Tussey. Back row, Bobby Marincil, Robert Blackburn, Pete Anderson, Ricky Dean, Kelson Littrell and Ernest Johnson. (Photo courtesy of Rhonda Meade Harmon)

For many years, Jim Van Zant was a respected sports editor at the *Williamson Daily News*. He is pictured here, in this early-1960s image, covering a local football game from the sidelines.

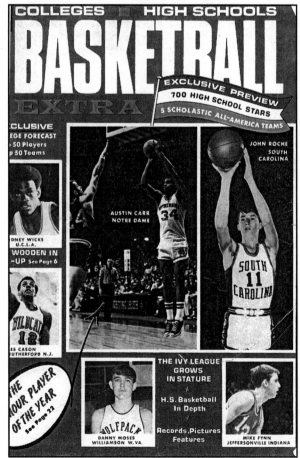

Here are some photos of Danny Moses, one of the top high school players in the country during his playing days. Moses, a 6-10 center, was one of the most highly honored and recruited players in Williamson High School's history. These photos show Moses during his Wolfpack days. He was an All-American and all-state performer during the late 1960s and early-70s. He was a 4-time all-area selection, 4-time all-state pick and 3-time All-American. He scored over 2,400 points in his career and during his senior season averaged 32 points and 17 rebounds per game. Moses first went to Wake Forest and later transferred closer to home to play at Pikeville College. He still holds the single game rebound record with 27 at Pikeville. During his high school playing days he rolled up impressive statistics. "Big Mo" brought a lot of exposure to Williamson. (Photos courtesy of the Moses family)

Here is the cover of a national magazine that shows Danny Moses, who was a 6-10 high school All-American in the late 1960s and early 1970s at Williamson High School. (Photo courtesy of Larry Moses)

In this tattered image, the Yanks Williamson Midget League baseball team from the early 1960s are shown. Front row, left to right, Kevin Hopkins, Rod McCoy, Randy Mcginnis, Dee Gentile, Billy Moses, Bernie Hubbard and Bo Gibson. Second row, Rick Cole, David Gillapie, Randy Runyon, Kenny Shelton, Flip Varney and Danny Moses. Back row, Coaches: Bo Gibson, Mr. Varney, Abe Hymore, Roland Hopkins, Ed Shelton, Paul McCoy and Sailor Runyon. (Photo courtesy of Danny Moses)

Chattaroy High School 1939 varsity team: Back row, left to right, Chafin, Richard Thompson, Irvin Smith, Preston Henry, Jack Cline and Carl Hofstetter. Front row, Lawrence Thompson, Howard Noe, Smith, Homer Davis, George White, and Coach Elmer Dickinson.

This photograph shows the Chattaroy High School team from the early 1950s. (Photo courtesy of Rob Harris)

This second image depicts four teammates on the Chattaroy High School team from the early 1950s. (Photo courtesy of Rob Harris)

At right, this is an action-shot of Chattaroy playing at Princeton. (Photo courtesy of Rob Harris)

This Chattaroy High School team in 1955 was the Class B state runner-up. The Yellowjackets, left to right, student manager Charles White, Earl Hensley, Steven Chafin, Buddy Pack, Jim Neace, George Ritchie, Johnny Teeters, Johnny Allen, Bud Burnett, Fred Vinson, Ray Elkins, Charles Teeters, Jim Alley and Coach John "Frog" Pinson. The team lost to Fairview in the championship game played in Morgantown by a score of 91-82. They were coached by John "Frog" Pinson and finished with a fine record of 21-6. (From the Fred Vinson collection)

At left, a CHS 1955 action shot from the state tournament shows George Ritchie (22) and Fred Vinson (30) on the right trying to stop a Fairmont player from driving to the basket. (From the Fred Vinson collection)

This image is another Chattaroy 1955 action photo from the state tournament. George Ritchie (22), Fred Vinson (30) and Earl Hensley (25) watch as a Fairmont player scores. (From the Fred Vinson collection)

The trophy presentation of the 1955 state Class B tourney between Chattaroy and Fairview. Chattaroy finished as the state runner-up. They lost in the championship game 91 to 82. (From the late Fred Vinson collection)

This photo shows the Chattaroy High School women's team from 1927. Back row, left to right, Mary Scott, Elizabeth Davis, Evageline Williams, Mae Scott and Coach Dove. Front row, unknown, Helen Giles, Irene Damron, Lena Estepp and Aileen Stepp. (Photo courtesy of Ed Goff)

This Chattaroy High School team was the 1962 Class A runner-up in the Mountain State. This is a partial team photo of that squad. Front row, left to right, Don South, Roger Jackson, Frank Smith and Doug Layne. Back row, Coach Bob Meade, Dodie Slone, Fred Campbell, Jim Webb and Roger Campbell. This team lost a tough game in the state championship to Williamstown by a score of 60-53. This was the last year of existence for the school. It was consolidated with Williamson in the fall of 1962. (Photo courtesy of Frank Smith)

Here is Chattaroy vs. Liberty Court action from 1959. Ed Goff is shown going up for a shot guarded by Roosevelt Gaither (43) and Steele (42). Also seen from CHS is Bill Keaton (23) and Curtis Bolden (20) of the CHS Yellowjackets. (Photo courtesy of Ed Goff)

At left, here is a photo from that splendid 1962 season for the Chattaroy Yellowjackets. The team went to the finals of the state tournament that year. Unfortunately they lost to a tough Williamstown. They had beaten Ronceverte in the semi-finals 78-55. The state tourney was played in Morgantown that year. In this photo Coach Bob Meade talks to Don South in front of the bench during a game. (Photo courtesy of Frank Smith)

This photo pictures three CHS players including Smith (30), Roger Jackson, middle, and Doug Layne. (Photo courtesy of Frank Smith)

Frank Smith (30) goes in for two in the semi-final win against Ronceverte. Chattaroy High School's cheering section was selected as the top in the state during the tourney. (Photo courtesy of Frank Smith)

Chattaroy's Doug Layne (31) goes in for a basket during the 1962 season. (Photo courtesy of Frank Smith)

This *Williamson Daily News* photograph shows coach Bob Meade talking to Roger Jackson and Dodie Slone. Jackson was a high-scoring guard, while Slone was the point guard. Slone was one of the best point guards in history to play for the Yellowjackets. (Photo courtesy of Frank Smith)

One of the unique stories that came out of Chattaroy's trip to the state tournament was the appearance of two Yellowjacket cheerleaders in a Morgantown newspaper. There were not many hotels in the Morgantown area at that time. Therefore many families played host to cheerleaders and players who had made the trek north. Margaret Spano and Geraldine Martin were featured in photos discussing how they stayed with a host family. The duo stayed with the Pinkney family. They received transportation to the games by a local auto dealership. These photos show the pair registering with the chamber of commerce and getting ready to be chauffeured to a tourney game by a salesman from the dealership. (Photos courtesy of Margaret Spano Pinson)

This classic image is of the Chattaroy High School football team from 1924. The team was coached by Adolph Hofstetter. Pictured are, front row, left to right, Millard Diamond, George Stepp, Bill Gaal, Harvey Kidwell and Roy Jarrell. Second row, l to r, Harvey Grabor, Ben Millard, Hayden Wellman, Ogal Ward and Hofstetter. Third row, l to r, Lee Smith, Martin Hofstetter, Tom Stepp and Millard Lowe.

Above, the Chattaroy High Cheerleading squad from 1962 included, pictured here, Geraldine Martin, Louise Politino, Linda Spano, Joy Chapman, Margaret Spano and Dana White. Linda Spano, at left, is pictured receiving the award for the most valuable cheerleader during the state tournament held in Morgantown that season. (Photos courtesy of Linda Spano Leonard)

This photo is of a girl's softball team from the Chattaroy Hollow area in 1960. The team was undefeated and won the City League championship. The group was sponsored by Spano's store. Back row, left to right, coach Don Anderson, Back Row, Judy Fletcher, Carol Campbell, Nancy Luther, Faye Johnson, Liz Chapman and Kay Finley. Front Row, Shayde Chapman, Margaret Spano, Louise Politino, Ellen Johnson, Bay Politino, Gussie Keaton and Joy Chapman. The team went undefeated that year. (Photo courtesy of Margaret Spano Pinson and Ed Goff)

This softball team is from Chattaroy in 1961. The team was sponsored by the old Hubbard Motors automobile business at Fairview. (Photo courtesy of Margaret Spano Pinson)

Burch High School won its first state title in 1957 in the old Class B division. This is a classic picture of that team. Number 60 in the back is of John Maynard, who came back to coach Burch in the 1970s and 1980s. Maynard coached the Bulldogs to a state Class A title in 1989. They beat Barracksville 58 to 54 in the championship game of the state tourney. Others on the team included Eddie Mick, Ronnie Floyd, Larry Mayhew, Bill Baker, Ed Starr, Wendell Wallace and Jim Browning. The squad was coached by Bill Young. Maynard, Mick and Floyd made the all-tournament team at the state tourney played at Huntington's Memorial Fieldhouse. Burch was the first high school from Mingo County to win a state basketball title. (Photo courtesy of John Maynard)

Lenore High School team of 1960, the Rangers, won the Class AA state title in 1962. Many of these same players were on that team. Left to right, front row, Coach Bob Meade, Lossie Mahon, Doug Lambert, Bob Davis, James Napier, Jerry Meade and Ray Lambert. Back row, James Brinegar, Bob Deskins, Doug Sorrell, Ken Maynard, Lewis Dobbins and Curtis Evans. Mahon went on to become a teacher and principal at Lenore. Maynard coached the Rangers in the late 1960s and 1970s. (Photo courtesy of Lossie Mahone)

At right, this is the 1972 Matewan High School basketball team. They finished as Class AA state runner-up. Coached by Joe Clusky and assistant coach Dick Montgomery, the team featured two all-state and all-area performers — Mike Collins and Billy Roberson — Jo Jo Clusky was the point guard. Other starters on the team were Herkie Estepp and Eddie Hamilton. Pictured above, front row, left to right, Steve Cunningham, Randall Williams, Eddie

Blankenship, Bobby Ferguson, Jo Jo Clusky, Eddie Hamilton and Herkie Estepp. Back row, asst. coach Dick Montgomery, Jessie Daniels, Mark Estepp, Billy Roberson, Mike Collins, Larry Curry and head coach Joe Clusky. Collins and Roberson both went to WVU. The Tigers lost a heartbreaker in the finals to Mullens 46-41. Mullens had upset Northfork in regional action to make it to the state tournament. (Photo courtesy of Mike Collins)

Kermit High School had one of the best teams in the state in 1964 regardless of classification. They won the Class A state title and finished with an undefeated record of 27-0. They beat Barracksville in the championship game 92-90. Kermit stayed undefeated beating Conley in overtime in regional action 74-70. They got by a tough Northfork-Elkhorn team in the regional finals. Only four teams made it to the state tourney in each class at that time. The Blue Devils defeated Paw Paw 94-72 in the semi-finals in the state tourney played in Morgantown. Members of the team in no particular order included Joe (Spaulding) Dingess, Herschel Sartin, Lewis Hale, Larry Weddington, Bill Parsley, Odell Sartin, Kent Hoke, Dick Goff, Teddie Parsley, D. Sone and B. Maynard. This outstanding squad was coached by Boyce Preece. All five starters averaged in double figures for this high scoring, fast paced team.

Kermit High School led by their passionate coach John Preece won the Class A state title in 1975. The school only graduated about 25 students in its senior class. Three members of that team went on to become medical doctors including J.W. Endicott, Bruce Hensley and John Carey. Kermit finished with a record of 22-4 and won the title game 48-37 over Piedmont. The Blue Devils defeated Matoaka in the semi-finals. Other members of the team were Guy Dillon, Barry Richardson, Cletus Sartin, Tim Webb, Lucky Stepp, Manny Rose, Jeff Kirk, Keith Brumfield and Billy Reeves. The assistant coach was Kent Hoke. (Photo courtesy of Anna Mae Sartin-Wellman and Dr. J. W. Endicott)

Most of the same players from the Kermit state championship team from 1975 are pictured above as junior high players at Kermit. This was taken in 1971. (Photo courtesy of Anna Mae Sartin-Wellman)

the 1950 Kermit High School team. The town of Kermit certainly supported its high school basketball teams over the years. The small Class Single A school won two state championships, one in 1964 and the other in 1975. But in 1950, Kermit High School's basketball squad was also the Class B runner-up. Byron "Wendy" Thornton, a longtime businessman and civic leader from Kermit played on this team. The Blue Devils were coached by Virgil Hoke. They beat a good Ravenswood team in the semi-finals 58-56, but lost in the championship to Athens 61-57. Members of the team are pictured above, front row, left to right, Charles Lambert, John Preston, James Bud Parsley, Glen Smith, Clarence Kirk and Coach Virgil Hoke. Back row, Jim Short, Jim Clay, Joe Porter, Billy Ray Kirk and included leading scorer Glenn Smith, John Preston, Jim Short, Charlie Lambert, Clarence Kirk, Thornton, Parsley, Clay and Byron "Windy" Thornton.(Photo courtesy of Windy Thornton)

Williamson High School's "glory years" were in the mid 1960s. The Wolfpack won the Class AA state basketball championship in 1964 and a state baseball title in 1965. Here are some pictures of those teams. The next season the school moved up to Class AAA and went undefeated until the final game in the state tourney, narrowly losing to Beckley. Counting the seven straight basketball wins the previous year in 1964, going 26-0 before losing in the final game, Williamson won 33 straight games, which is thought to be the best in school history. The Pack also won the state baseball tournament that first year in Class AAA. Many of the same players who suited up on the basketball team also played on the baseball squad. The basketball team was coached by George Ritchie, while the baseball team was coached by Cecil Hatfield. The Williamson High School team of 1964 was the Class AA state champs in basketball in West Virginia. This was the school's first state title on the hardwood. Pictured, front row, Doug Layne, Johnny Brooks, Greg Slater, Freddie Campbell and Bill Craig. Middle row, Harlan White, James Young, Buster White and Clarence Chapman. Back row, holding the sign, Ivan Albert and A. J. West. The Pack beat Summersville in a romp in the semi-finals by a score of 89-59 and they defeated Magnolia 80-68 in the state championship game. It was nothing for this balanced squad, who really came together down the stretch run of the season, to have four or five players score in double figures each game. Brooks, Greg Slater and Layne made the all-tourney team. In one game Slater was a perfect 7-7 from the field, a state record he held for many years. This same year Kermit won in Class A and Logan in Class AAA, giving the southern coalfields all three state champs in roundball. All of the schools were within a 50 mile radius. (Photo courtesy of Bill Craig)

The 1962-63 team was the fist at Williamson High School that featured players from Chattaroy, after the two schools consolidated. Pictured, front row, Ivan Albert and Herschel Allison. Middle, seating, left to right, Bill Craig, Robert Foglesong, A. J. West, James Young, Dodie Slone and Fred Campbell. Back row, standing, assistant coach Ben Hamilton, Jimmy Webb, Donald South, Johnny Brooks, David York, Doug Layne, Tom Pertee and head coach George Ritchie. (Photo courtesy of Bill Craig)

The 1965 team at Williamson moved up in classification from Class AA to AAA and went undefeated until losing the final game at the state tournament. This is arguably one of the best teams to ever take the court for the Wolfpack. They went 26-1 and were rated No. 1 by the UPI in West Virginia during the regular season. The team had to win a tough regional over Huntington and did so 88-80. They then won the regional crown in a triple overtime thriller against Stonewall Jackson of Charleston 65-62. In the state semi-finals they beat Triadelphia 72-61, however lost a heartbreaker to Beckley Woodrow Wilson 69-67 in the championship game. Pictured, front

row, Wayne Levy and Ivan Albert. Sitting, left to right, Tennis Mahone, Buster White, David Tincher, Robert Wright, Mike McBrayer, Curt Fletcher, Terry Looney and Greg Slater. Back row, assistant coach Ben Hamilton, John Yost, Bill Craig, Paul Layne, Clarence "Pee Wee" Chapman, Jack Maynard, Don Skeens and head coach George Ritchie. Not pictured, Mike Slater. White, Greg Slater and Craig made the state tournament all-tourney team. This Wolfpack squad finished the season with a 25-1 record. (Photo courtesy of Bill Craig)

Pictured here is Freddie Campbell, Jimmy Webb and Charles Hoback in the early 1960s at Chattaroy High School. (Photo courtesy of Linda Spano)

This is an early 1950s photo of Chattaroy Junior High School's basketball squad. Pictures, Pete Campbell, J.C. Haney, Edgar Cox, Raymond Snodgrass, Richard Roberts, Jimmy Kohari, Earl Hensley, Dan Estepp, Joey Kohari, George Ritchie, Sam Cassidy, James Collins, Don Marcum, Bill Keaton, Charles Curry, Ray Cundiff, Paul Slater, Robert Merencis, Charles Teeters, H.C. Justice, Jackie Webb, William Fitch and Coach Charles Hale.

This photo was taken at the 1937 Williamson Kiwanis Club basketball tournament. The image shows both players and fans in the old WHS gym. (Photo courtesy of Linda Spano)

Here is a photograph from 1921 of one of the first football teams at Williamson High School. The coach was Everett Howton. Some of those identified in the photo include No. 2 Tony Gentile. He went on to become the football and basketball coach at Williamson. Others on the team were No. 9 Bill Cantees and his brother No. 16 Sam Cantees. No. 4 Tabor Ball and No. 3 Jack Sampselle were also identified. (Photo courtesy of Jeanette Cantees McCoy)

Frank Wolfe was the first Williamson football coach. From his name is where the school nickname came from, The Wolf Pack.

The above photo is of the basketball team sponsored by the YMCA in East Williamson. Back row, left to right, Danny Smith, Jim McNamara, Gene Hensley and D. L. Darby. Front row, Roy Lee Marcum, Hugh Frazier, Gardner Scott, Joe Ferris and Blaine Pruitt. (Photo courtesy of Jeff Hensley)

This is a photo of a Williamson youth team sponsored by the N & W Railroad. It was taken in the early 1940s. (Photo courtesy of Jeff Hensley)

DICK HENSLEY
End—New York Giants
Age: 22; Residence, Raleigh, N. C.
Height: 6-4   Weight: 210

During earlier part of rookie season, 1949, filled in wherever required—offense or defense. Came on fast at season's end. Finished as regular offensive right end. Standout performer for University of Kentucky in the tough Southeastern Conference. Opposed many of his present team mates. Out of football 1 year before becoming a pro.

No. 184 in a SERIES OF FOOTBALL PICTURE CARDS
© 1950 Bowman Gum, Inc., Phila., Pa., U. S. A.

Here is a football card of Dick Hensley, who played on the 1944 state championship team for Williamson High School. Hensley went on to play for the University of Kentucky and then the New York Giants in the early days of the NFL. Also, here is a copy of the schedule from that 1944 Wolfpack team. (Photo courtesy of Jeff Hensley)

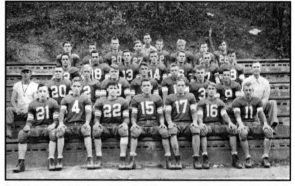

This is a youth baseball team from East Williamson. Dick Hensley of Williamson was a standout athlete. His nephew, Jeff Hensley, also played football at Williamson High School in the early 1970s. This team is believed to have been sponsored by the N & W Railroad (Photo courtesy of Jeff Hensley)

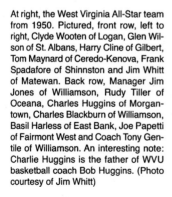

Doug Long, Freddie Caudill, and Gene Chamberlain are shown working out during the summer months at the old softball park by the West End swimming pool. All were standout athletes, and the three played for Williamson High School in the 1950s.

The Matewan High School Football Team poses for this photograph in 1950. (Photo courtesy of Jim Whitt)

At right, the West Virginia All-Star team from 1950. Pictured, front row, left to right, Clyde Wooten of Logan, Glen Wilson of St. Albans, Harry Cline of Gilbert, Tom Maynard of Ceredo-Kenova, Frank Spadafore of Shinnston and Jim Whitt of Matewan. Back row, Manager Jim Jones of Williamson, Rudy Tiller of Oceana, Charles Huggins of Morgantown, Charles Blackburn of Williamson, Basil Harless of East Bank, Joe Papetti of Fairmont West and Coach Tony Gentile of Williamson. An interesting note: Charlie Huggins is the father of WVU basketball coach Bob Huggins. (Photo courtesy of Jim Whitt)

This West Virginia All-Star team has some familiar and famous faces. In the back row, number 12 is Jerry West, who went on to become a legend at WVU, as well as in the NBA. Also, front row, number 7 former Chattaroy and Wake Forest star George Ritchie, who came back to coach at Williamson High School in the 1960s and 1970s. Number 14 in the back is Willie Akers, who played at WVU and later coached at Logan High School. Number 3 is former WVU player and longtime Mountaineer radio color commentator Jay Jacobs. Other players in the photo are Mickey Neal and Carl Slone who played at Williamson High School and former Wolfpack coach Tony Gentile. Several other players from this team went on to play Division One college basketball. (Photo courtesy of the late George Ritchie)

The 1965 Williamson High School baseball team won the Class AAA state championship. Here is a team photo of that great squad. Many of those fine athletes are pictured here holding the trophy after winning the final game. They were coached by Cecil Hatfield. The WHS baseball squad was the state champions of West Virginia. Here is a photo of the trophy presentation after the title game. Also included is a complete team photo of that historic 1965 team. It includes, front row, left to right, Doug Dudley, Ronnie Ferrell, Freddy Peatross, John Reed, Mike Slater and Marvin Whittaker. Second row, Greg Hurley, Curt Fletcher, Richard O'Neil, Greg Neal, Terry Looney and Mike McBrayer. Back row, assistant coach George Ritchie, Greg Slater, Bill Craig, Tom McQueen, Tom Evans, Sonny Burmeister, Robert Wright and head coach Cecil Hatfield. (Photo courtesy of Bill Craig)

This image is of the 1939 Kermit High School basketball squad. (Photo courtesy of the Kermit Library)

Here is the 1937 Kermit varsity basketball team. (Photo courtesy of the Kermit Library)

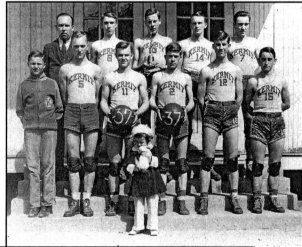

Here is the 1937 Kermit High School football squad. At one time Kermit had a powerful and successful football team. (Photo courtesy of the Kermit Library)

Above, here is the Kermit grid iron team from 1939. (Photo courtesy of the Kermit Library)

In the photo, left to right, was coach Tom Blankenship and players Jerry Scott and Ivan Browning, of the 1949 Matewan High School football team. (Photo courtesy of Jim Whitt).

JAMES RAMEY
DEFENSIVE TACKLE
HAMILTON TIGER-CATS, 1982

UNIVERSITY OF
KENTUCKY

1965 FOOTBALL FACTS
FOR PRESS·RADIO·TV

Two former Belfry High School standout football players, Rick Kestner and James Ramey, both went on to play for the University of Kentucky, and later in the NFL. Kestner, a tight end, who played in the early 1960s was drafted by the Baltimore Colts. Ramey, a defensive lineman, played for the St. Louis Cardinals and then in the World Football League and in the Canadian Football League. (Photos courtesy of Dave Damron)

This team photo of the American Legion Post 49 baseball team is from 1956. This team won the West Virginia state championship and went to the east regional of the national tournament. Pictured, front row, left to right, Kenny Sanderfur, Bobby Jones, Freddie Tiller, Frank Offutt, Streak Marenko, and Burgess Oliver (bat boy). Middle row, Donnie Oliver, Paul Neil Slater, Mickey Neal, Kenny Echols, Butch Beckett and Bobby Beckett (bat boy). Back row, coach Jim Van Zant, Carl Childress, Jim Keatley, Ronnie Floyd, Jim Clark, Ireland Smith and Ronnie Whitt. Larry Hall, who had broken his arm, was not pictured in this photo. The photo was taken on the wooden bleachers underneath the grandstand of Lefty Hamilton Park. Those unique and historic bleachers were destroyed by the 1977 flood. (Photo courtesy of Ireland Smith)

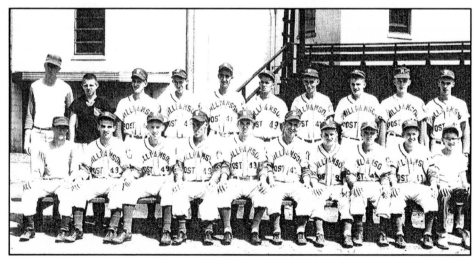

This is another team photo of the Post 49 team. Front row, left to right, Streak Marenko, Mickey Neal, Ronnie Floyd, Kenny Echols, Paul Slater, Bobby Jones, Fred Tiller, Ken Sandefur, Butch Beckett and Donnie Oliver. Back row, Coach Jim Van Zant, Bobby Beckett, Frank Offutt, Larry Hall, Carl Childress, Ronnie Whitt, Ireland Smith, Jim Keatley, Jim Clark and Donnie Oliver. Notice the old wooden grandstand in the background of the picture and part of the historic Williamson Fieldhouse. (Photo courtesy of Ireland Smith)

Above, the 1956 Post 49 baseball team is shown prior to boarding a train on their trip to Washington, D. C. for the national tournament. The man kneeling at the far right is "Chawkeye" Thurston, who was a well-known Williamson resident and baseball fan who followed the local sports teams. Fans raised money so that Thurston could travel with the team to the regional tourney. It is a well-known fact that Thurston was befriended by Stan Musial, who started his pro baseball career in Williamson. Musial would send tickets to Thurston so that he could travel to Cincinnati to see him play when the Cardinals would visit Cincinnati at old Crosley Field. Many residents have said that Musial would also send Thurston money, once he made it to the major leagues.

Here is the Chattaroy Midget League team from 1965. Pictured, front row, left to right, Michael Hatfield, Terry Taylor, Mike Howard, Doug Howard, Jimmy Fletcher, Gale Copley and Rickey Southers. Back row, Barry Copley, Gary Taylor, Jerry Southers, Marty Bo Copley, Larry Thompson, Ronnie Vanhoose, Randy Thompson, Gary White and coach A.J. West. (Photo courtesy of the Southers family)

This is a photo of the Williamson High School cheerleaders from 1956. Pictured, left to right, Sheila Watson, Beverly Lowe, Verla Grace, Martha Caudill, Carol Justice and Marsha Grace.

Jim Barnett of Chattaroy High School graduated in 1953. He was named "Big All-State" that season. He was the only player from a small school, Class B during that era. Barnett is said to be one of the best basketball players to ever suit up for the Yellowjackets. He was awarded a full scholarship to West Virginia University. Coach Red Brown touted the Mingo Countian higher than future hall of famer Hot Rod Hundley. A knee injury hurt Barnett's career at WVU, but he was one of the first players from the area to garner a scholarship to WVU. (Photo courtesy of Jim Barnett)

Jim Barnett earned his degree from WVU and got into coaching. His first stint was with WVU Hall of Fame coaching legend Fred Schaus. Schaus, who coached Jerry West and the Mountaineers during the golden era of the late 1950s, went on to coach in the NBA. He later came back to WVU as athletic director. Barnett is pictured with Schaus. He went on to coach for several years in Cincinnati, Ohio. After retirement he returned home to Chattaroy.

Many who live in the Tug Valley grew up listening to stories about St. Louis Cardinal great Stan Musial. Musial got his start playing for the Williamson Redbirds in the Coalfield League. He came down on a bus from Donora, Pennsylvania. He started out as a pitcher, but was later moved to the outfield because of his hitting. He is a member of the Major League Baseball Hall of Fame. Here, in this tattered photo, is an image of Musial in downtown Williamson with Graham Smith, J. Brooks Lawson, Jim Bero and Bill Osborne. Smith and Lawson both went on to become prominent lawyers in Williamson. The picture was taken in front of the courthouse in Williamson. (Photo courtesy of Bunkie Smith)

This autographed photograph of Stan Musial, at right, was signed during an early-1990s interview with the author. He had fond memories of his days in West Virginia, and spoke fondly of his two seasons playing in Williamson.

73

Two photos on this page, at right and below, show Coach Lefty Hamilton. The baseball field in West Williamson was named after Hamilton. He's credited with inspiring many players, and helping several make it to the next level. (Photo courtesy of Eddie Stogsdill)

Above, Nat Hickey played in Williamson and later went on to play in the early days of pro basketball for the Boston Celtics. He was an outstanding athlete who played in two different professional sports leagues. (Photo courtesy of Eddie Stogsdill)

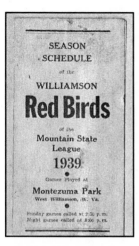

AT HOME		AWAY	
April 30	Logan	April 28, 29	Logan
May 3, 4	Welch	May 1, 2	Bluefield
May 5, 6	Ashland	May 9, 10	Welch
May 7, 8	Huntington	May 15, 16	Huntington
May 11, 12	Bluefield	May 18	Ashland
May 13, 14	Logan	May 19	Welch
May 17	Ashland	May 21, 22	Huntington
May 20	Welch	May 23, 24	Bluefield
May 25	Ashland	May 26	Ashland
May 27, 28	Bluefield	May 30	Logan
May 31	Huntington	June 3	Logan
June 1	Huntington	June 5	Welch
June 2	Logan	June 6, 7	Ashland
June 4	Welch	June 10, 11	Ashland
June 8, 9	Bluefield	June 12, 13	Logan
June 14, 15	Huntington	June 18, 19	Welch
June 16, 17	Ashland	June 23	Welch
June 20, 21	Logan	June 24, 25	Bluefield
June 22	Welch	June 26, 27	Huntington
June 29	Welch	June 28	Welch
July 2, 3	Ashland	June 30	Bluefield
July 4	Logan	July 1	Bluefield
July 6, 9	Huntington	July 5	Logan
July 10, 11	Bluefield	July 6, 7	Ashland
July 12, 13	Welch	July 14, 15	Huntington
July 17	Logan	July 16	Logan
July 18, 19	Huntington	July 20, 21	Ashland
July 20	Logan	July 22	Logan
July 26, 27	Ashland	July 24, 25	Welch
August 2, 3	Logan	July 28, 29	Bluefield
August 5	Welch	July 30, 31	Huntington
August 6, 7	Bluefield	August 4	Welch
August 8, 9	Welch	August 10	Logan
August 11	Huntington	August 12, 13, 14	Ashland
August 16, 16, 17	Bluefield	August 23	Huntington
August 18, 19, 20	Ashland	August 24, 25	Welch
August 21, 22	Huntington	August 27, 28, 29	Bluefield
August 26	Welch	August 30, 31	Huntington
September 1	Huntington	September 4	Logan
September 2	Welch		
September 3	Logan		

A front and back copy of the Williamson Redbirds schedule from 1939. Before the team was an affiliate of the St. Louis Cardinals, the minor league team was known as the Williamson Colts. (Photo courtesy of Eddie Stogsdill)

The May Brothers of Pond Creek had their own baseball team. The team consisted of nine brothers. This photo shows the brothers and their parents. From left to right, is the father, Basil May, and sons Dare, Roland, Wardy, Mose, Doc, Buford, Sherman, Blaine, Bob and their mother, Dixie. The photo was taken in 1937 in front of the Mingo County Courthouse, according to family members. (Courtesy of Ronnie May)

This photo is of the Majestic-Freeburn Industrial League baseball team. Front row, left to right, is Manager Carl Biliter, Lawrence Mounts, Monk Dotson, Thomas Lewis, and Eugene Ingersol. Back row, left to right, Ralph Dado, Jack Fannin, Ernie Moore, Jack Cunningham, Clyde Fannin, Bill Fowler and Elbert Murphy. (Photo courtesy of Yvonne DeHart)

The photo at left shows the Ransom, KY, Coalfield League baseball team. (Photo courtesy of Yvonne DeHart)

The 1946 Coalfield League baseball team, sponsored by Howard Collieries Mine of Chattaroy is shown at right. The late James "Homer" Davis, who was a member of the team and the author's uncle, identified the individuals. Front row, left to right, unknown, Paul Kirk, Jim Mamone, Homer Davis, Wayne Noe and James Southers. Back row, Ott Haney, Jack Robinson, Ray Moody, Dick Hensley, Ed Slone, Bud Wynn, Sam Spano, Sr. and P. J. Wynn. (Photo courtesy of Don Davis)

CATCHER
DOC EDWARDS

Howard "Doc" Edwards, a catcher from Red Jacket, made it to the major leagues after playing in the Coalfield Leagues in the late 1950s. He also played at Matewan High School. This is a picture of his Topps baseball card. He played for the Athletics and Indians, and after his playing days, he later became the manager of the Indians. He managed and coached in the minor leagues for several years. This is his Topps Baseball Card from the 1960s.

This photo shows Doc Edwards with Evelyn Steele Ferrell. It was taken in Cleveland as the A's were in town to take on the Indians. It was taken by her husband, Sid Ferrell, who grew up on Pigeon Creek. Doc went to Red Jacket Junior High with Evelyn, who also grew up on Beech Creek. She was the daughter of Harry and Belle Steele. The photo was taken on Fan Appreciation Day. (Photo courtesy of Brenda Sampsel)

Rocky Marciano, who went on to become the heavyweight boxing champion of the world, played one summer in the Coalfield League. He was a catcher. Marciano originally wanted to become a baseball player, but fate chose a different career path for the eventual boxing champ. He was the only undefeated heavyweight championship with a 49-0 record.

This image is of the Williamson Colts minor league baseball team. Before the Williamson team became affiliated with the St. Louis Cardinals and garnered the nickname Redbirds, they were an independent squad known as the Colts. (Photo courtesy of Eddie Stogsdill)

Above, the Majestic Coalfield League baseball team from 1930-31 is depicted in this photo. Pictured, left to right, E.C. Lewis, Majestic Superintendent, Joker Hall, Cat Ford, Russell Wakeland, John Fannin, Mike Emody, Andy Emody, Shirely "Pickle Beans" Slone, Ernest Hensley, Bob Bowman, Clyde Lewis and Stewart "Tuff" Jones. Both Slone and Bowman went on to pitch in the major leagues. Slone with St. Louis and Bowman for St. Louis and the New York Giants. (Photo courtesy of Bob Fannin)

Here is one of the only known photographs of Stan Musial when he played for the Williamson Redbirds. (Photo courtesy of the late Charlie Blevins)

The 1948 WHS baseball team won the state championship. All-State players on the squad were Bob Stultz, Billy Gene Hall, Gaston Jude, and John Lee Chapman. The state championship trophy was presented to Jude by a state tournament official.

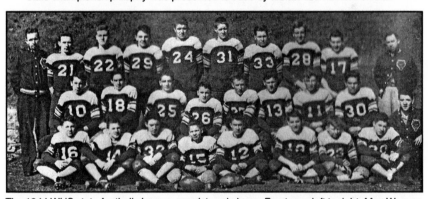

The 1944 WHS state football champs are pictured above. Front row, left to right, Max Weaver, Frank Tsutras, James Farley, David Schroder, Rexal Jackson, George Wilburn, Paul Adkins, Don Bradley, and Frek Linkenhoker. Middle row, Fred Adams, Donald Swartz, Barnes Gillespie, Don Smith, Ralph Adkins, Jack Lipps, Henry Hatfield, and Abe Hymore. Back row, Coach Marvin Varney, Greenway Hatfield, Ray Moody, Ivan Weaver, Dick Hensley, John Persinger, Frank Moricle, Arnold Kenly, Dick Bradley, and Ast. Coach John Pinson.

Here, the 1961-62 WHS state football champs are pictured. Back row, Jim Taylor, Noah Brunty, Bobby Gene Oliver, Jim Ader, Donnie Faith, Alonzo Pinson, Freddie Oakes, Colin Berry, David Whitaker, Gary Levy, Tubby Farley, and Roy Wilson. Front row, Jim McQueen, Ron Wooten, Roscoe Blackburn, Jerry Ferrell, Thomas Mills, Clifford Marenko, Rusty Thompson, Duffy Reed, Wallace Cleary, Terry Tackett, and John Elliot. Standing to the left is head coach John Moricle and to the right assistant coach Ike Weaver.

Flooding in Tug Valley

The April 1977 flood was perhaps the most devastating disaster in the recent history of the Tug Valley. The Tug Fork River continued to rise to record levels after several days of rain. Many think the long, cold and very harsh winter played an important factor in the spring flood. Millions of dollars in damages were done to homes, businesses, schools and other structures along the Tug River and its tributaries. Unbelievably, no one lost their life during this flood. But many people were rescued by neighbors, first responders or volunteers. It took weeks, months and even years for the area to rebound.

The water in downtown Williamson reached an estimated fifty-seven feet. The muddy water got as far as Fifth Avenue. In years past, the water had only flooded downtown Williamson, and had reached the lower section of Third Avenue and the Harvey Street underpass.

Smaller towns like Matewan and Kermit, and every small community in between was affected by the raging water. Entire homes and other structures floated off their foundations. Cars and debris were washed down river. The aftermath brought in the U. S. Army, the National Guard, the American Red Cross, The Salvation Army, HUD officials and government officials.

The following pages show many pictures of the event during and after the horrific flood hit the Tug Valley basin.

Williamson

Williamson lost many businesses and there were millions of dollars worth of damage within the business district. Many believe the county seat was never the same after the flood. Yet, the citizens bounced back and continued to move forward. Just seven years later in 1984, another flood hit the area. It was not quite as big, but the muddy water still did its damage. The current floodwalls were eventually built for Williamson, West End, South Williamson and Matewan. Some homes in the outlying areas were eventually bought out by the U. S. Army Corp of Engineers, while others were raised up on blocks out of the flood zone.

(Many photos in this section from the late Graham Smith collection, with special thanks to his wife, Bunkie Smith. Other submissions by Williamson Library).

Matewan

Matewan was hit hard by the flood of 1977. The town sits right along the Tug Fork River and had been flooded several times in the past. This time the flood nearly wiped out the town.

Nolan

I grew up in Nolan and still lived there with my father in 1977. I recall that I barely made it home from Williamson as the flood waters rose the night before. In fact, I had to go through back water at Peter Street in East End as I went "around the loop" trying to make it home. I drove through heavy runoff at two other locations before making it home. My car died out three times from moisture in the distributor cap. I eventually made it home. The next morning when Dad woke me, it was hard to believe how high the water had risen. It was at record levels at that point, and continued to rise the rest of the day. Like others in the community, I helped people evacuate from their homes later that morning. The small town of Nolan was hit hard and, like most communities along the river basin, was virtually destroyed.

Here are some photographs that I took with a small Kodak camera. Although the quality wasn't the best, I knew at the time I was capturing history. Some of these, like the boat tied up to the bush, were taken from my front porch. The basketball goal you see in a couple of the photos was mine. Those were also taken from my front porch.

Falls Branch

The 1977 flood was devastating to the entire region, and Falls Branch
was also hit hard by the flood waters.

Kermit

The Town of Kermit sits on the northern most border of Mingo County. Since they are down river, Kermit was the last town to get swallowed by the rising waters of the Tug. Record flood levels also hit this community, and these images show the water over the businesses, city hall, and fire department. (Photos courtesy of George and Bobbie Marcum of Kermit)

Besides the 1977 flood, the Tug River overflowed its banks many times over the years. Two of the bigger floods were in 1957 and 1963. Here you'll also find a photo from the George Marcum collection of the flood from 1957 at the mouth of Marrowbone Creek, north of Kermit.

94

Memories of Nolan

The small hamlet of Nolan is located within the heart of Mingo County, in the cradle of the Appalachian Mountain range. Its location is approximately eight miles north of the City of Williamson. In this section, memories are shared and history is documented through a variety of vintage images from the region.

This is the railroad bridge at Nolan, which is still in operation. It remains the route for the railroad to bring coal out of the Big Creek area of Pike County, Kentucky. Even though it was technically and legally off limits, and not open to pedestrian traffic, many used the bridge to travel across the Tug River to Martin County, and to Big Creek. Many have said that, by using the bridge, one can walk in two states—and into three counties—within the span of five minutes.

This photo is of Slone's Grocery, operated by Tom and Gertie Slone for many years, and later by their son Tommy Slone. At one time, there were as many as four grocery stores operating in Nolan.

This image is of Kyle Lovern, uncle of the author, with a female friend. It shows part of the old train depot at Nolan in the background. At one time, about every town along the railroad line had its own passenger and freight train station.

This image is of Sam Lovern, father of the author, and his older brother, Kyle, sitting on the family's mule at their farm in Nolan. A large wooden barrel beside the house was used to collect rain water. The image is circa 1914.

Curry's Restaurant was a popular hangout for families and young people at Nolan, where they whiled away the hours playing pool or pinball games, dancing, and courting.

This image is of Gladys Lovern with her cousins in front of the water well at the Lovern homeplace. Gladys' father, Samuel J. Lovern, Sr., (also father of the author,) was known by many as 'Uncle Sam' and was one of the early founders and settlers in the community of Nolan. Below center, Samuel J. Lovern, Jr. is shown during the World War II era. Like many Mingo County residents, he served proudly. Lovern was awarded three Bronze Stars and served in New Guinea and the Philippines in the South Pacific Theater. The small town of Nolan had several young men who went into the armed forces.

Above, this aged professional photograph is of John Kelly Lovern, of Irish ancestry, and the great-grandfather of the author. He is pictured here with his wife, Catherine (Kitty) Hall Lovern. The couple were some of the earliest residents settling into the region near the community of Nolan. Circa, 1890.

This barn was located at the Harris farm near the community of Nolan, at the mouth of Big Creek on the other side of the Nolan Toll Bridge. In the early 1960s, besides traditional farming, the Harris family sold sweet-churned homemade cow butter and fresh eggs to residents in the community.

At left, Rose Mary Francis stands near the entrance to the Kentucky side of the original Nolan toll bridge, which was a swinging bridge used by both automobiles and pedestrians. It was eventually replaced by a sturdier structure in the mid-1960s. The concrete piers from the original still stand. (Photo courtesy Rose Mary Francis)

In the early 1990s, when the state was constructing U.S. 119 (Corridor G), road planners came through Nolan, Miller's Creek, and Borderland. In doing so, planners discovered an Indian mound located near the riverbank and train tracks at the mouth of Millers Creek, shown above, and archaeologists eventually excavated and removed the burial grounds. When the discovery was first announced, Native Americans protested the disturbance or removal of the mound and its skeletal remains. Eventually, an agreement was reached with the Native American group and its removal took place (shown below). This story made state and national news.

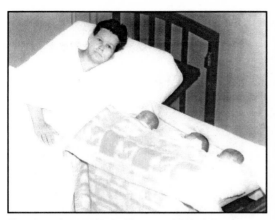

Here is a photo of Vada Pinson and her triplets born at Williamson Memorial Hospital. It's believed these three were the only triplets ever born in Mingo County. The three sons were named Moses, Otis, and Thomas. Their father was John "Tom Dick" Pinson, who was a longtime Boy Scout leader and softball coach in Nolan. Below, another photo of the Pinson triplets. (Photo courtesy of Margaret Spano Pinson)

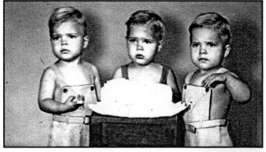

The photo above was taken in front of the Nolan Theater. It shows five teenage girls in front of theater marquee. In the front row Yvonne Blevins Marcum and Gail Copley; back row, unknown, Becky Marcum, and Dorothy Marcum. The building was later used as the Bluegrass Palace Tavern. (Phot courtesy of Fred Vinson collection)

This snapshot, at right, taken on the Nolan Railroad Bridge, is of Raymond Taylor, Lowell Dove, and Check Vaughn. The bridge seemed to be a common meeting place over the decades, and was often used by pedestrians to travel across the river. (Photo courtesy of Donna Taylor Goble)

Many individuals remember the Red Robin Inn, owned and operated by the equally memorable Charlie Blevins, shown at right. The Red Robin was a popular watering hole in the Nolan area. Known locally as a favorite "beer garden," the Red Robin was built by Blevins, who was well known for collecting old antiques. He was also known far and wide for his talent of strumming his unique groundhog-hide banjo. Through the years, many other musicians played and sang at the bar, as well.

Below, Charlie is shown here sitting on the stoop of the Red Robin a few months before the building was sold to the highway department for demolition.

Wallace "Wally" Marcum was a longtime deputy sheriff in Mingo County, and a basketball coach, who lived in the Big Splint section of Nolan. He also served in the U. S. Navy during the Korean Conflict.

This photo, taken in the early-1930s, shows William "Bill" Allen at the local airport at Borderland, known as "Airport Bottom." At the time this photo was taken, bi-planes occasionally landed at the airport with a grassy-field landing strip. The hangar on the grounds is located in the background of this image on the left. Allen later died from an accidental drowning in 1934. (Courtesy of Ed Goff)

Like a scene from Tom Sawyer, friends Donnie Taylor and Clinton Whitt are shown swimming in the Tug River at Nolan. The stream was a popular fishing and swimming spot for youngsters in and around the community. (Photo courtesy of Donna Taylor Goble)

Freda Sorrell Taylor and Jean Taylor Smith are shown on the railroad bridge at Nolan.

Above, S. J. Lovern, Sr., known as Uncle Sam to townsfolk in Nolan, is pictured here with his wife in the early 1950s. He was a respected member of the community and one of the early settlers of Nolan and Big Splint.

In these tattered photos from yesteryear, above and at right, several students are shown outside the wood-framed Nolan School House. The time period was the early-1920s. Kyle M. Lovern, the author's uncle, is shown in the photos along with several members of the Chapman family.

This is a snapshot of a Sunday School class at Nolan. The teacher was Sylvia Persinger, and four of the children were sisters, Polly Jane, Liz, Shayde, and Joy Chapman. (Photo courtesy of Donna Taylor Goble)

This rare photo shows friends, Joey Kohari and Ray Elkins, photographed near Nolan, on their way to school. Kohari later became a magistrate in Mingo County. (Photo courtesy of Ray Elkins)

Town of Matewan

The Town of Matewan has a colorful and important history. A proud community with equally proud inhabitants, Matewan is located close to the Tug River in Mingo County and remains the home of many who have lived in the region for generations. Of course, nowadays it's a modern and growing community with a rich heritage. It's oftentimes associated closely with the history and the participants of the Hatfield and McCoy Feud, and is also connected with long ago labor issues and union struggles. In this section, a variety of rare images from the community of Matewan are displayed.

This photograph was contributed by former Matewan Mayor Johnny Fullen. The image shows a copper still, distillation supplies, and glass jars of illegal liquor stacked up in front of the Matewan City Hall building after the illegal liquor operation was discovered and confiscated by local law enforcement. The youngsters standing behind the bottles are the mayor's relatives, Dave and Curtis Brown. This image was taken around 1932 (the last year of Prohibition) by Mayor Fullen's grandfather, John W. Brown. During this period, especially during the Prohibition years, moonshine stills and illegal mason jars of "white lightning" were commonplace within the county's borders.

At the time this photo was taken, the Brown family owned a dry cleaning business next to City Hall. During his tenure in office, Mayor Fullen also led the community in the preservation and restoration of many of the town's oldest buildings.

This aged and tattered photograph, which was once used as a postcard, is of the old Buskirk Bridge in downtown Matewan. The postcard was from 1918. (Photo courtesy of Yvonne DeHart)

This photograph is of the E.B. Chambers Dealer and General Merchandise Store in downtown Matewan. The general store served the community and residents living in the rural area surrounding the town, and featured dry goods, clothing, shoes, hardware and groceries. At the time this photo was taken, most citizens still traveled by horse and buckboard wagon. It's likely that many of the Hatfields, participants of the Hatfield and McCoy feud, shopped at this location for their staple items, such as flour, coffee, and sugar. This photo was probably taken around 1915. (Photo courtesy of Yvonne DeHart)

Above, the Matewan City Hall block building and Lock-Up still stands in the community of Matewan. The Lock-Up was used to hold temporary prisoners or publically intoxicated residents, or to incarcerate criminals until they could be transported to the jail at the county seat. Originally built in 1901, Matewan City Hall had many historical figures pass through its doors over the years. At left, Fred Hatfield stands near the gas pumps at the Amoco Gas Station in Matewan. (Photo courtesy of Yvonne DeHart)

Local residents lined up for a photograph in front of this old carry-out located near the town of Matewan. The one-story, one-room general store served its community in the 1930s and 1940s. (Photo courtesy of Yvonne DeHart).

The WHJC studio on "Radio Hill" in Buskirk is known as Matewan's only radio station. Its once broadcast only Gospel Music in the early days, and later added Country and Western music. It aired live church programs and live entertainers, too.

Matewan Mayor Cable Testerman was gunned down during the explosive shootout at the 1921 Matewan Massacre.

This picture, at right, displays some of the bullet holes left during the violent Matewan Massacre in 1920 that left several Baldwin Felts detectives and Mayor Cable Testerman dead. This battle made a hero out of Police Chief Sid Hatfield, shown below, who sided with striking coal miners trying to organize the union. Hatfield's grave marker is located across the Tug River on the hillside above the community of Buskirk, KY.

BRASS PLUGS ABOVE MARK BULLET HOLES LEFT BY MAY 19, 1920 BATTLE OF MATEWAN

In this worn photograph, Matewan Police Chief Sid "Two Gun" Hatfield, also known as "Smilin' Sid," is shown demonstrating his fast-draw. It's been written that it was the famous gun battle at the Matewan Massacre that gave Hatfield a degree of national celebrity. However, following the massacre, he was keenly aware his life was in danger from Thomas Felts, of the Baldwin and Felts Detective Agency, who sought vengeance for the killing of his brothers, Albert and Lee. Sid was later indicted on murder charges stemming from the Matewan shootout and was eventually acquitted by the jury. He was later sent to stand trial with his friend and deputy, Edward Chambers, on conspiracy charges for another incident in Welch, WV. Both men arrived in Welch on Aug. 1st, 1921, unarmed. Several Baldwin-Felts men shot them on the McDowell County Courthouse steps. Hatfield died instantly. Chambers was also killed that day. None of the Baldwin-Felts detectives were convicted of Hatfield's assassination, and claimed they had acted in self-defense.

The Hatfield Family. Front row, left to right: Tennyson "Tennis" Hatfield, son of Anderson Hatfield; Levicy Hatfield, daughter of Johnse Hatfield; Willis Hatfield, youngest son of Anderson Hatfield; and "Watch" or "Yellow Watch," Anderson "Devil Anse" Hatfield's coon and bear dog. Second row: Mary Hensley-Simpkins-Howes, daughter of Anderson; with daughter, Vici Simpkins; family patriarch Anderson "Devil Anse" Hatfield; Louvicey Chafin Hatfield, wife of Anderson; Nancy Elizabeth Hatfield, wife of Cap Hatfield, with son Robert Elliott Hatfield; Louise Hatfield, daughter of Cap Hatfield; Cap Hatfield, second son of Anderson Hatfield; and Coleman A. Hatfield, son of Cap Hatfield. Top row: Rosa Lee Hatfield, daughter of Anderson; Detroit "Troy" Hatfield, son of Anderson; Betty Hatfield Caldwell, daughter of Anderson Hatfield; Elias Hatfield, son of Anderson Hatfield; Tom Chafin, nephew of Anderson Hatfield; Joe D. Hatfield, son of Anderson Hatfield; Ock Damron; Shephard Hatfield, son of Cap Hatfield; and Levicy Emma Hatfield, daughter of Cap Hatfield.

This image is of feudist and family patriarch Anderson "Devil Anse" Hatfield (in his last years) standing beside Willis Hatfield, Louvicey Hatfield, John Caldwell, Betty Hatfield Caldwell, and Joe Hatfield; the children are Osa and Joe Caldwell. Circa 1919.

Randall "Ol' Ran'l" McCoy, the patriarch of the McCoy family lived on the Kentucky side of the Tug River. Long before the Hatfield and McCoy clash began, it's believed that Ran'l McCoy and Devil Anse Hatfield were friends and once even cooperated in the 1863 assassination of General Bill France of the Kentucky Home Guard during the Civil War. In later years, Randall lived in Pikeville and operated a meager ferry business.

Anderson "Devil Anse" Hatfield was the patriarch of the Hatfield clan and lived on the West Virginia side of the Tug River. He was once captain of the Logan Wildcats, a local militia group during the Civil War. In 1865, it's believed that Devil Anse, along with Uncle Jim Vance, was involved in the assassination of Asa Harmon McCoy, brother of Ran'l McCoy. Some believe this was the act that eventually fueled the famous feud between the Hatfields and McCoys.

The Magnolia Fair has been held for many years in Matewan. During the early years it was held at O'Brien Park, the old football field. This is one of the carnival rides from the early 1960s. (Courtesy of Yvonne DeHart)

This Red Jacket Coal Company mining photo was taken outside the deep mine on August 17, 1939. Posing before work are the crew members from the Junior Mine day shift, top seam, Red Jacket Coal Corp. Front row, Ed Gillespie, Reed Maynard, Tom Chafin, John McGinnis, Elmo Charles, mine foreman Dan Hammond, Lawrence Price, Henry Varney, unknown, Louie Rebick. Second row: unknown, Lee Canada, Kenneth Rowe, Andy Maynard, Clarence Watkins, Tom Blankenship, unknown, Lee Mahon, Bill Richmond. Third row: Charlie Richmond, Ira Simpkins, Wirt Cook, Frank Hammond, unknown. Fourth row: Ivan Meade, unknown, Steve Collins, Jack Doyle, Glen Hammond, John Halley, Wally Hatfield, Tommy Kinder, Frank Melmige, Jones Canada, Walter Simpkins, Nicholas Hatfield, Dudley, Bred Charles, Alfred Peters, Manuel Barrios, Elliott Simpkins, Elmer Long, Jack Simpkins, Roscoe Hatfield, unknown, Kennedy, Dow Blankenship, unknown, unknown, unknown, unknown, Herbert Wiley, unknown, Albert Burgraff (center of photo) Arthur Fitzpatrick, Johnnie Burgraff, Jim Backus, Jess Otom, John Kyle, Norse Vance. Fifth row: unknown, Theiskel Fitzpatrick, unknown, unknown, Wayne Simpkins, Harry Charles, Russell Williamson, Joe Murphy, unknown, unknown, unknown, McKinnley Daniels. Sixth row: unknown, unknown, Alvin Harmon, unknown, Doc Johnson, unknown, W. J. Brown, unknown, Milton Hodge. Seventh row: Lee Chafin, William Whiteside, Ray Simpkins, Troy Maynard, Scott Simpkins, Med Kennedy, Dow Blankenship, unknown, unknown, unknown, unknown, Herbert Wiley. Eighth row: General Superintendent of both seams of Junior Mines A. F. Cook, unknown, Edgar Maynard, Buster Varney, Harry Steele, Earl Wallace, Frank Mahon, Willard Hatfield, Ralph Staten, Braxter Skeens, Vernon Mitchell, Earl Rutherford, Tony Sanito, Stewart Osborne, Campbell, Chandis Simpkins, Linkous Cisco, Earl Looney, Tennis Hatfield and Luther Blankenship. (Photo courtesy of Debbie Fuller Rolen)

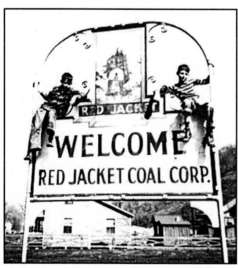

These two youngsters climbed atop the Red Jacket Coal Company sign near Matewan. The coal company was a major employer in the Matewan area.

A mounted Baldwin and Felts Detective Agency detective is shown here during the time of the Matewan Massacre.

This photograph, likely from the late-1940s, is of a traveling coffee salesman for the Standard Coffee Company. At the time, the Standard Coffee Company provided commercial coffee products for many of the restaurants in the region. Pictured on the left is Merrell Bentley. At right is salesman Leonard Estepp. (Photo courtesy of Yvonne DeHart)

Estil Hatfield, a well-known native of the Matewan and Williamson area, is pictured in front of the old country store on Beech Creek. Hatfield was known for playing Bluegrass music in the area. (Courtesy *Williamson Daily News*)

In this photograph, residents pose in front of the Blue Goose Saloon, operated at the time by R.W. Buskirk, in downtown Matewan. The local business was a popular gathering place prior to Prohibition. The child carrying metal pails in the foreground is likely delivering buckets of warm beer to community residents, which was commonplace for saloons at the time.

This image is of the Matewan Train Depot in the downtown area along the railroad tracks. Today, an exact replica of this depot has been rebuilt using the original railroad blueprints in its construction. The Matewan Depot is open to the public and is now a local museum and tourist attraction.

The Town of Matewan and, at right, the Matewan Train Depot. Circa 1920s.

An impressive wooden structure, the Thacker Train Depot was located just south of Matewan. Most towns and hamlets along the steam railroad line had their own depot or train station, built by the railroad company. The design of this structure looks much like the depot that was also in Matewan (See above and on page 116). Dry goods, groceries, home furnishings, iron cookstoves and appliances, general merchandise, and mail bags were transported and shipped into and out of the community by rail at the time. Circa 1920s.

Other Great Communities
Kermit, Dunlow, Naugatuck, Dingess, Crum, Chattaroy, Delbarton, and Lenore

The next pages focus on the people and the communities of Kermit, Dingess, Crum, Dunlow, Naugatuck, Lenore, Delbarton, and Chattaroy, all located within the borders of Mingo County. Like many other communities in Southern West Virginia, these small towns—some beginning as only small clusters of frame homes—were inhabited by hard working families that were carving out an existence in a foreboding and rugged land. As you turn the page, you'll find vintage images from yesteryear that evoke fond memories and document important history.

An amazing engineering feat for its day, Dingess Tunnel, nearly one mile long, was completed in 1910 and was originally used as part of the railroad line to move bituminous coal and raw timber out of northern Mingo County. This vintage photograph, above, shows some of the laborers, which included European immigrants and African Americans, who dug the tunnel—most of it done by hand and using early steam shovels—through the mountainside located near Laurel Lake. The old tunnel is still used today as a passageway for automobiles and trucks moving through the county (shown at right.)

119

These images portray the train depots at Crum (above photo), Kermit (bottom photo), Dunlow (middle right photo) and Lenore (middle left photo). Most of the small towns throughout the area had "whistle stop" depots. Early train travel was one of the ways families traveled to Williamson and Logan to buy provisions for the month. (Photo courtesy George and Bobbie Marcum collection)

The Log Cabin Tavern and Restaurant at the junction of U.S. 52 and Route. 65 in Naugatuck was a popular eatery in the 1950s and 1960s. (Contributed by Ann Damron)

In this photo, the White Family gathered for the image in the Lenore area. (Ann Damron collection)

This photo shows a Mingo County family outside the Parsley General Store in the Lenore area. (Ann Damron collection)

This log cabin once sat in the bottom across from Lenore, located at the current site of Lenore Middle School.

This image is of children playing in Kermit in the 1930s. At the time, the Town of Kermit was a growing community. (Photo courtesy of George Marcum)

In this worn image, coal camp frame houses were being constructed in Stepptown, just north of Kermit on U.S. Route 52. Coal camps, built and maintained by local coal companies, were commonplace in the region from the early-1920s through the 1950s, providing housing for coalminers and their families. Mining companies also provided company stores, community churches, civic buildings, and boarding houses in the camps. (Photo courtesy of George Marcum)

Jack Dempsey, former heavyweight boxing champion of the world, once lived in Holden, a coal camp in neighboring Logan County, and had relatives who lived in Mingo County. After leaving the area and becoming a boxer, he came back to visit the region several times. He once put on an exhibition fight in Williamson for charity. These pictures, above and below, show Dempsey when he was in the prime of his career. (Photo courtesy of the late Charlotte Sanders)

Above, in this image from 1956, former heavyweight boxing champion of the world is pictured with several Mingo County children. Below, while visiting the region, Dempsey met with several Lenore residents, including Walter Copley, Frank Blair, and Fred Blair. Dempsey is second from the left. (Photo courtesy of Ann Damron)

This image is of Chattaroy hollow in the early years. Loaded train cars can be seen at the left side of the photograph. This photo is believed to have been taken in the 1920s from atop a hill looking down on Chatttaroy. Like many coal towns of the time, it was a thriving coal community. (Courtesy of Don Davis and Ed Goff)

This rare photograph shows some members of the Howard Colleries Safety Club, from the Howard Colleries Store. The employees are, left to right, Jack Martin, Ray Estepp, unknown, unknown, Roy Estepp, and unknown. Rube Dingess may be one of the unknown individuals. (Courtesy of Ed Goff)

Howard Colleries Store was located across the bridge from Chattaroy High School. The building later became a popular restaurant and hangout for teenagers.

This special dedication was held at the Chattaroy Church of God, a block structure located near the mouth of the hollow. The time period was not given on this image, but it may have taken place in the late-1940s or early 1950s. The importance of faith and church attendance has always been important to many in this part of Mingo County. (Courtesy of Don Davis)

This snapshot was taken at the Chattaroy Confectionery in 1928. The image originally appeared in the *Williamson Daily News,* and was taken by Fannie Williamson, wife of Floyd Williamson. Pictured, from left, are Dave Sublett, Charles Foster, who was the owner of the store, Lee Smith, Mae Foster, Floyd Williamson, and Jim Foster. The sign to the right advertises "Talking Pictures" at the Cinderella Theater in Williamson. (Photo courtesy of Ed Goff)

Here is the old grocery and dry goods store, called Hatfield's General Store. It was located at the mouth of Chattaroy Hollow, on the left after one crosses the railroad tracks. The store kept livestock and chickens in the fenced areas in front of the store. The store was a landmark in the community for many years. (Photo Courtesy of Ed Goff)

The three photos on this page were taken of a train wreck at Falls Branch near the mouth of Chattaroy hollow. The tangled wreckage, which included several loaded coal cars and freight cars, can be seen in the images from the early-1950s disaster. (Courtesy of Ed Goff)

The Borderland Tipple was located along the Norfolk and Western railroad tracks just north of Chattaroy and south of Nolan. This was a well-known landmark and major employer in the Tug Valley for many years. (Photo Courtesy of Ed Goff)

In this 1953 image, Boyd Maynard, a Delbarton police officer, poses in front of the town theatre, often called the Dell Theater. The marquee promotes a double-feature: "Killer Ape," with Johnny Weissmuller portraying Jungle Jim; and "The Moonlighter," a Western featuring actor Fred MacMurray. (Photo courtesy of Bert Staton)

Davis Cash Store, a local grocery, is shown in the background of this image from the main street of the Town of Delbarton. Clifford Davis, at right, a longtime insurance salesman and civic leader, holds his daughter, Cathy. Others in the photograph are Nancy Davis, Jerry Davis, and Jewel Davis. This was taken around 1956. (Photo courtesy of Bert Staton)

Glenn Roddy is shown at the old Pure filling station located across from Delbarton Grade School. Circa 1950s. (Photo courtesy of Bert Staton)

School Teacher Effie Davis, at left, stands with her students at the Elk Creek Grade School, a one-room school house, located near Delbarton. (Photo courtesy of Yvonne DeHart)

The historic Elk Creek Bridge has been an attraction and landmark for many years. The structure was used until the 1990s, and was originally built during the Roosevelt administration.

This image shows a busy intersection in downtown Delbarton. The main street of the community is a part of State Route 65 toward the left. Straight ahead is the community of Ragland.

Railways, Coal Industry, and Timber Business

Some historians believe the modern age came to Southern West Virginia at the point passenger and freight trains first arrived in the Appalachian Mountains. Prior to tracks being laid in Mingo County, hand-cut logs, household provisions, and other products were transported by river barges (often with industry having to wait to transport merchandise up-river during the rainy seasons); or, merchandise was moved across the mountain ridges with timber sleds or wagonloads drawn by teams of muscular pack mules. With the arrival of the steam locomotive, in both Logan and Mingo Counties, transportation became more robust, efficient, and practical. New employment opportunities came to the region. And, at the same time as the arrival of railways, coal-mining emerged as a massive industry for the region. Simultaneously, the local timber industry grew in scope to meet these new demands that came from the arrival of coal companies.

There were great passenger trains of yesterday with names like Powhatan Arrow and Pocahontas. For years the trains were pulled by steam engines, like the 611 above, and were commonplace in Mingo County.

The powerful Powhatan Arrow is shown belching clouds of steam as it rolls through Stonecoal in the early 1960s. (Photo courtesy of George Marcum)

The massive steel wheels of the 611 engine are shown here in the Williamson train yard.

The mighty 611, with smoke belching from its smokestack, rolls through the Norfolk and Western yard in the county seat.

The panoramic view shows the Borderland No. 2 coal company and tipple in the early days of the Twentieth Century. (Charlie Blevins collection)

This image is of Borderland Tipple with its long conveyor running across the Tug Fork.

This image of this steam locomotive was photographed at Glen Alum in 1891.

It was Friday, August 14, 1914, when five armed gunmen, believed at the time to be members of the "Black Hand" or "Italian Mafia," attacked a small payroll handcar on the four-mile railroad spur from the N&W railroad's main line to the coal camp of Glen Alum. The men in this photo represent the Glen Alum posse that eventually captured and killed the robbers. The full payroll was also retrieved. (*Williamson Daily News* photo)

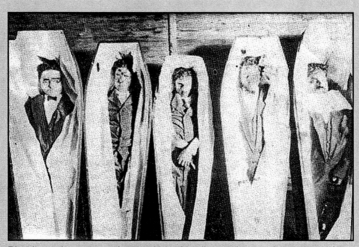

Bloodhounds were used to track the bandits, and several posse members were killed during the manhunt. The Glen Alum robbers, after being shot and killed by Mingo County posse members, were put on display in their caskets. In all, eleven individuals died for a payroll of around $7,000. The robbers were never identified, and some accounts at the time said their bodies had been mutilated by some members of the posse. (*Williamson Daily News* photo)

The images on this page depict the massive train wreck that took place in 1950 at Glen Alum in southern Mingo County. The wreck, where many loaded coal cars were overturned, happened near the coal tipple. (Courtesy of Carol Sue)

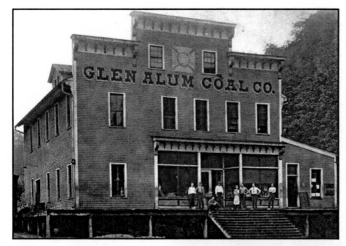

The Glen Alum Coal Company Store building was located in rural Mingo County near the McDowell and Wyoming County line. Over the years, many coalminers and their families were served at this store.

Island Creek Coal miners are shown here entering a deep mine in Mingo County. Island Creek Coal Company was one of the largest coal operators in the region for many years. They had several mines throughout the region.

Julius Lawson, Jr. is shown working underground at Lackey Coal Mine in the 1950s.

137

The Lick Creek tent colony is shown here during the mine wars. This location is on Route 49 between Williamson and Matewan. Many tent communities were organized after coal company barons evicted striking miners from their coal company houses. Labor strife in the region was not uncommon as miners struggled for unionization. (Photo courtesy of Yvonne Dehart)

Striking miners gather for a snapshot at a Lick Creek tent colony. Tent homes can be seen in the background. (Photo courtesy of Yvonne Dehart)

This is an aerial view of the roundhouse at the Williamson location of the Norfolk & Western rail yard.

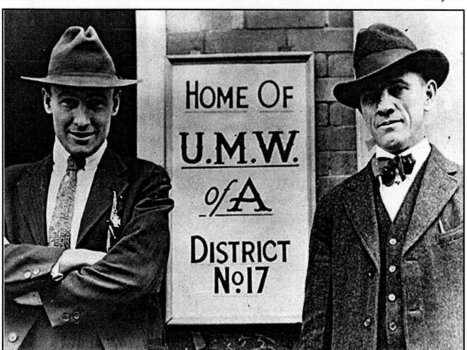

UMWA organizers are shown in this image from the early days of District 17 in Mingo County.

An engineering party for a local coal company was being held when this image was taken. The snapshot was taken in front of the Wharncliffe Train Depot.

A typical company store building from the early 20th century, this was located in the heart of coal country, in Mingo County. (Photo courtesy of Yvonne Dehart)

Two photos, above and below, show the brick Sycamore Company Store building at Cinderella. The above photo is from the 1940s. The building is still standing up Cinderella Hollow, just south of Williamson. (Kyle Lovern collection)

In the fall of 1921, United States soldiers and armed guards, along with heavy military equipment, rolled into the train yard in Mingo County at a time when local coalminers were striking and the UMWA was again trying to organize in the area. The guards and military personnel came into the region to restore order in the coalfields at a time when violent skirmishes like the Matewan Massacre and the Blair Mountain War had already made national headlines.

At the height of the Mountain State mine wars, this photo shows a Mingo County tent colony where coalminers and their families temporarily lived. The miners and their families were evicted from coal company "camp houses" because the miners were accused of trying to organize a union in the coal-fields.

The City of Williamson N & W Train Station was a busy hub for passenger and freight transport. Passenger train travel was especially popular during the first half of the 20th Century,

This is a photo of miners and their families at the UMWA Miners Community Center building located in South Williamson. Circa 1940s. (Photo courtesy of Ron Blackburn)

Memories of Tug Valley

In this section, photographs are offered from all areas of the county—of people, places, and activities—that represent special moments, unique landmarks, and fond memories of our region.

Many people recall the old road which was often referred to as "going around the loop" from East End, by Cinderella, over Sycamore Mountain, and down through Chattaroy, and back to U.S. 52. There were three sycamore trees that automobiles passed three times due to the curvy engineering of the roadway. On the Chattaroy side of the road was Kewanee Park, a popular picnic spot that many families and church groups used through the years. It was eventually taken over by a trailer park after the 1977 flood and then sold to the current 84 Lumber Company.

Blaze Starr, the famous exotic dancer, was born Fannie Belle Fleming and was raised at Wilsondale, near Dingess, in Mingo County. She was born January 1, 1932, and is known as an American burlesque star. Her life story was relived in a bestselling book, and later portrayed in a major motion picture, *Blaze*. Starr left her Mingo County home as a teenager and eventually moved to Baltimore, Maryland, where she began performing at nightclubs in the 1950s, eventually becoming a headline act. Starr's striking red hair and voluptuous figure was part of her great appeal. She still occasionally visits family in the region. (Photo courtesy of Bennie Fleming)

On April 19, 1939, AM radio station WBTH took to the air at 6:00 a.m. in the morning. The station, broadcast 1,000 watts during the day, 500 watts after sundown. It would go off the air nightly as the broadcast silenced at midnight. This picture is of Bob Stanley in the old studio in the Mountaineer Hotel. (Courtesy of Jimmy Wolford)

This winning bowling team proudly displayed their trophies from a Williamson bowling alley in the early-1960s. Some of those in the photos are Guy Klucker, Roland Staten, Jelly Akers, and Babe Akers. The photo was provided by Louise Staten Hughes, and Roland Staten was her brother.

This Boy Scout troop posed for this image in the mid-1960s. The photo was provided by Natalie Young of Williamson. Her father, Andy, and uncle, Billy Ray, are two of the scouts. The late Dr. Tchou, who was later killed in a plane crash after taking off from the Mingo County Airport, was the troop leader and is pictured in the back row. Others in the photo include Rachel Tchou, Michael Tchou, Ruth Murphy, and Richard Murphy.

The Mingo Oak, a great white oak, was once a legendary local landmark and was said to have been the largest white oak tree on record. It was later cut down in 1938 after fumes from a nearby coal refuse pile damaged the tree. It was cut down by a special crew from Webster County. The lumber that was harvested from the tree was used for various items, including a church pew that rested in one of the older churches in Williamson. The Mingo Oak stood near the head of Trace Fork of Pigeon Creek, near the Logan-Mingo County line. It is estimated that the tree was over 100 years old. On many Sabbath days during the summer and early fall, rural ministers gathered their followers to conduct religious services beneath the oak. It has been estimated that more than 500 sermons were preached at the location. (Photo courtesy of Yvonne DeHart)

Music has always been important to the people of Mingo County. This image is of the late Frank Hammond, once an accomplished local Bluegrass musician that frequented local festivals and played at many venues over the years.

This image is of a local musical group, "The South Sea Dreamers." At the time, these members called themselves radio and recording artists. They, like many local entertainers of the late-1940s era, played live shows at WBTH radio and at other locations throughout the county. (Courtesy of the Williamson Library)

In the 1960s, Country Music legend Loretta Lynn performed in Williamson on several occasions. The popular singer, from nearby Butcher Holler in eastern Kentucky, packed the Cinderella Theater when this photo was taken. The promoter for the concert was local musician Jimmy Wolford.

A young Tanya Tucker, wearing black, performed in Williamson in the 1970s when she was just starting her career. She went on to have many top hits on the Country Music charts. Tanya is pictured here with John Phillips and York Smith (far right), constables during the era. (Photo courtesy of York Smith)

Once a common site in Southern West Virginia, this outdoor toilet was located near the mouth of Cinderella Hollow. It was located behind an old house along U.S. 52.

Above, correctional officer William "Mooch" Justice is shown on the left. Standing, Bill Hill, a teacher who also taught GED courses to local inmates, is shown with former Deputy Sheriff Wally Marcum, seated on the right. The image was taken in the Mingo County Courthouse.

Anna Mae Sartin Wellman, a councilwoman from Kermit, provided these photos of her grandfather, Anthony Wayne Brewer, the father of Sanford Brewer. According to Wellman, Brewer was one of the first West Virginia State Troopers assigned to Mingo County. He is pictured alone, above, in his uniform, and with some other troopers, at right, at Matewan. (Photo courtesy of Anna Sartin Wellman)

Former *Williamson Daily News* reporter Charlotte Sanders, who spent over sixty years with the local newspaper, is pictured in this image with Fred Nicewonder, Clarence Booth, and Mr. Lindsey. They were each presented awards for their exhaustive work with the United Fund, a local organization that raised monies for non-profit groups such as the Boy Scouts, Girl Scouts, American Red Cross, and other non-profit groups. (Courtesy of the *Williamson Daily News*)

This photograph was taken at the Red Robin Inn. In the front, from left to right, is Carbide, Kentucky Slim, and Charlie Blevins. Carbide was known in the region for driving around the region with a huge speaker attached to his vehicle. Using the speaker, he would loudly announce advertisements for local politicians. In the background, behind the bar, is local musician and songwriter Glen Simpson.

Andrew "Tug" Herald is shown holding his child, Lafayette Herald. Beside him, on his left, is his wife, Callie Lowe Herald. Herald was responsible for installing some of the first phone lines in the Tug Valley. Circa 1918. (Photo courtesy of Natalie Young)

Constables Raymond Fitch, Mont Howell, and Earl Daniels are shown shortly after they confiscated a moonshine still in Mingo County. Constables played an important part of law enforcement in the county. (Photo courtesy of the Mingo County Sheriff's Department)

Fred Mickel, of Williamson, once ran Mickel's on Second Avenue. He is pictured here during Williamson's Centennial Celebration in 1963, in which the men competed in a beard-growing contest. Many women of the town dressed up as pioneers, as did this unidentified woman with her bonnet and apron.

Teenage friends, Glen Sammons, Fred Caudill, and David Blevins, are shown in this image "horsing around" in downtown Williamson in the mid-1950s.

Maude (Sloan) Matney is shown milking a cow. Circa 1935. (Courtesy of Robin Croaff)

This snapshot of Bill Croaff and his horse, "Maude," was taken at Glen Alum around 1948. (Courtesy of Robin Croaff)

Breeden resident Harmon Stroud is shown in the mid-1930s with his horse. (Courtesy of Robin Croaff)

Several ladies at a local bowling league pose for this photograph in early-1961. This was taken at the Pike-Mingo Lanes at Goody, KY, located just past Williamson. (Photo courtesy of Wilma Jean Martin)

Students at Chattaroy High School pose for this image in the 1960s during a Sadie Hawkins Day festival. (Courtesy of Linda Spano)

This Appalachian Power Company Christmas Party was held in Williamson in the early-1960s. (Courtesy of Rhonda Meade Harmon)

This image shows *Williamson Daily News* employees and some of their family members. The editor of the newspaper at the time was Dutch Tolbert. Circa, late-1950s.

At left, Rimer Stissel, a *Williamson Daily News* employee, is shown operating a linotype machine at the newspaper office in the early-1960s. At the time, linotype operators had to be accomplished typists, mechanics, and machinists, as well. Stissel worked for the local newspaper for nearly 50 years.

Tom Wellman, center, was a longtime news reporter and photographer for the *Williamson Daily News.* Wellman also took photos at local weddings and other events in the Tug Valley area for many years. Pictured with Wellman is Mark Russell, left, a local attorney and former prosecutor and, right, Lafe Ward, a Williamson attorney and former state senator.

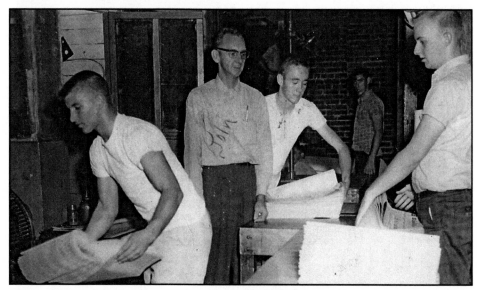

In this image from the 1950s, *Williamson Daily News* Circulation Manager John L. Burris, center (wearing glasses,) oversees several pressroom employees as they catch newspapers coming off the press. The papers were later counted and tagged for delivery.

In this image from 1976, railroad passengers are shown boarding an Amtrak car at the Williamson Train Station located on Fourth Avenue. For years the Norfolk & Western ran passenger trains through the Williamson yard.

L.P. 'Barney" Harvath, left, was the general manager and publisher of the *Williamson Daily News* for several years. He is pictured with Howard Stallard as they review the latest edition to roll off the press in the early 1960s.

Charlotte Sanders, shown in an image from the late-1950s, was a highly respected reporter at *Williamson Daily News*. She spent parts of seven decades working for the daily newspaper and covered thousands of stories over her long career. She was also considered Mingo County's historian.

Former pressroom foreman Howard Stallard, at left, is pictured at the *Williamson Daily News,* working beside Ronald Blackburn. This photo is from the early-1960s.

The N & W General Foreman's Office was located in Williamson. Circa 1920s.

This image was taken in 1950 at the Williamson Railroad Station.

A local landmark, this 1928 photograph is of the U.S. Post Office in Williamson.

Here, in this early photograph from the downtown streets of Williamson, city workers prepare the roadway for paving. This photo is believed to be from around 1915, and most of the city streets were paved with red brick at the time.

Politicians, Civic Leaders
and Dignitaries

This section of this volume focuses on the people, the leaders, and the dignitaries that have shaped Mingo County over its history.

Standing, from left to right, Marc Russell, Lafe Ward, Harry Artis, Noah Floyd, Steve Adkins, and William F. "Dutch" Tolbert. Tolbert was the longtime editor of the *Williamson Daily News* in the 1950s and '60s. These Williamson civic leaders went to Washington, D.C. to meet with U.S. Senator Robert C. Byrd to seek flood protection for the town. (Courtesy of Bill Tolbert)

Senator John F. Kennedy spent many days in southern West Virginia campaigning for the 1960 Democratic Primary. This photo shows JFK shaking hands with a resident in front of the Hobbs "five and dime" store. (Courtesy of Jimmy Wolford)

Mingo County legislators stand behind West Virginia Gov. Arch Moore. Governor Moore is shown handing Mike Whitt, far left, who was a member of the House of Delegates at the time, the ink pen he had just used to sign a piece of legislation. Also, left to right, Jim Reid, Ken Hechler, H. Truman Chafin, John Pat Fanning, and A. James Manchin look on.

Local civic leader Mae Stallard, standing at left of the microphone, is shown presenting an award to Brooks Lawson, an attorney in Williamson. Tug Valley Chamber of Commerce director Archie Bowen is shown standing in the middle. This was during one of the early King Coal Festivals in the City of Williamson. Stallard is one of the driving forces behind the AIM Group that organized the annual festival held each September. Circa 1970s.

This photo from 1965 shows several well-known politicians from Mingo County during the era. Back row, standing, left to right, Lafe Ward, Steve Adkins, Ernest Ward, Harry Artis, Tom Chafin, and O. T. Kent. Front row, sitting, left to right. Wade Bronson, unknown, T.I. Varney, unknown, Noah Floyd, and Fred Shewey.

Dr. H.D. Clark was presented the Key to the City of Williamson by Mayor Sam Kapourales. (*Williamson Daily News*)

Former Williamson Mayor Sam Kapourales is shown with Dr. H. D. Clark, a longtime Williamson dentist, Harry Joyce, and Billy Lee. The mid-1970s meeting was for a city proclamation for Black History month. (*Williamson Daily News*)

Former Williamson City Clerk June Blevins is pictured at left, former mayor Sam Kapourales in the center, and the late Alex "Poochie" Bucci, a longtime police officer for the city and a bus driver for Mingo County. They are shown at a city council meeting in the 1970s.

Former Congressman Ken Hechler, who later ran for governor of West Virginia and served as Secretary of State, is shown campaigning in the City of Williamson. He was known for driving his famous red Jeep around the state during his campaign trips.

Former Mingo County Magistrates Bill Webb and John Moses are shown being sworn into office by Judge Spike Maynard in this mid-1970s image.

Late Williamson attorney Brooks Lawson is shown presenting the Kiwanian of the Year award to John Messerian.

Former Williamson Mayor Sam Kapourales speaks to the Williamson Rotary Club. Hobart Hamilton, former Rotarian and manager of the old G. C. Murphy Store in downtown, is shown at the far left.

United Fund chairman Charlie Albert is shown with Professor F. Dean Lucas of Southern West Virginia Community College, at right. Albert raised thousands of dollars annually for non-profit organizations in the Tug Valley. He was also a longtime Rotary Club member and founding member of the club in Williamson.

In the 1970s, civic leaders in Mingo County included, left to right, Clarence Booth, Estil "Breezy" Bevins, Don Campbell, and Ron Rumora. Bevins also served as a city council member and mayor of Williamson. This photo was taken in the courthouse after a donation was made to the OH9 Ambulance service. These men were on the board of directors.

At right, James "Buck" Harless (center), an entrepreneur from Gilbert, is shown with Gov. Arch Moore. Over the years, Harless has donated millions to education in Mingo County and to both Marshall and West Virginia Universities. *(Williamson Daily News)*

In this photo, Buck Harless, businessman and entrepreneur from Gilbert, is shown receiving a local award. The self-made millionaire has been honored many times for his charitable donations. (*Williamson Daily News*)

In 1966, Robert C. Byrd spoke at the Lebanese-Syrian Convention in Williamson. His beloved wife, Emma, is shown at his right. (Photo courtesy of Jeanette Cantees McCoy)

Local civic leader Nick Maroudas, a longtime pharmacist, is pictured in this 1970s-era photo. Maroudas was a former city council member and is a loyal sports booster for Williamson athletics. He is pictured with longtime Hurley Drug employee Kathy Hardin.

Longtime United Fund volunteer John Ramey is pictured at right. He worked for Cotiga Land Company in Williamson. He is pictured with former Delbarton Fire Chief Denny Lemaster.

Williamson's Jimmy Wolford, at right, is shown with former U.S. Senator from Minnesota and Vice President Hubert H. Humphrey. A former singer and entertainer, Wolford campaigned with Humphrey when the Minnesota senator ran for the Democrat nomination for president in 1960. On the campaign trail, Wolford would entertain crowds and serve as master of ceremonies at rallies across the country. This image shows Humphrey looking at one of Wolford's 45-rpm records he released in the early-1960s. Wolford and Humphrey became good friends through his campaign efforts. (Photos courtesy of Jimmy Wolford)

Jimmy Wolford helped presidential candidate Hubert Humphrey pack in the crowds on the campaign trail in 1960. Wolford served as emcee for the U. S. Senator from Minnesota. Wolford later helped campaign for JFK, as well, after Humphrey was defeated in the primary election. Wolford rubbed elbows with many artists and actors and played venues across the country, including Las Vegas. Some of his early songs, recorded in the early-1960s, made the Billboard charts. (Photo courtesy of Jimmy Wolford)

Roy Taylor was a Williamson banker who also served as city mayor for several years from 1970 to 1979. He is pictured here at his Williamson office. (Photo courtesy of Charlotte Sanders)

This image is of U.S. Senator Robert C. Byrd with this book's author. Senator Byrd was in Williamson for a dedication ceremony. During his career, Byrd brought millions of dollars into Mingo County for various projects including Corridor G (U.S. 119,) the floodwalls in Williamson and Matewan, and many other important undertakings.

Radio personalities John Moses and Jimmy Wolford are shown during a WBTH radio remote in downtown Williamson in the mid-1960s.

About the Author:

Kyle Lovern is a longtime journalist in southern West Virginia, working in both newspaper and radio. As an award-winning writer and reporter, his work has been published in a variety of forms and publications.

His expertise is as a news reporter; yet, he has also covered county and state sporting events and, for many years, served as a popular newspaper columnist in southern West Virginia and Eastern Kentucky.

His features, articles and photographs have been published in *Golden Seal Magazine, Wonderful West Virginia Magazine,* and other distinguished publications.

He is also the author of *Appalachian Case Study: UFO Sightings, Alien Encounters and Unexplained Phenomena, volumes 1 and 2.*

Lovern was born and reared in rural Mingo County, West Virginia, in the small community of Nolan. He is a graduate of Williamson High School, Southern West Virginia Community College, and Bluefield State College.

He and his wife, Vicki, reside in Williamson, West Virginia. They have three grown children and three granddaughters.

Other Exciting Book Titles By
Woodland Press

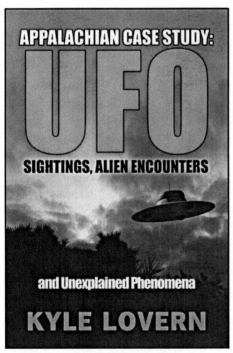

APPALACHIAN CASE STUDY

Softcover. 108 Pages.

The Appalachian region has a long prominent history of unexplained happenings and bizarre sightings of unidentified flying objects (UFOs). People share their actual experiences in this first volume. By Kyle Lovern.

APPALACHIAN CASE STUDY VOL. 2

Softcover. 170 Pages.

An amazing journey of exploration through the eyes of many Appalachian citizens who tell about their UFO sightings, encounters, and experiences. Appalachian Case Study, Volume 2. Softcover. By Kyle Lovern.

A Step Back in Time
TRIADELPHIA DISTRICT
LOGAN COUNTY, WEST VIRGINIA

Pictorial History Researched and Organized by
Members of S.T.A.R.T.
Seniors Taking Active Roles Today

A STEP BACK IN TIME

Softcover. 178 Pages.

Here is the history of Triadelphia District—communities like Man, Rita, Yolyn, Dehue, and others—in Logan County, West Virginia. It covers the past through rare images and words. Over 300 vintage photographs and images.

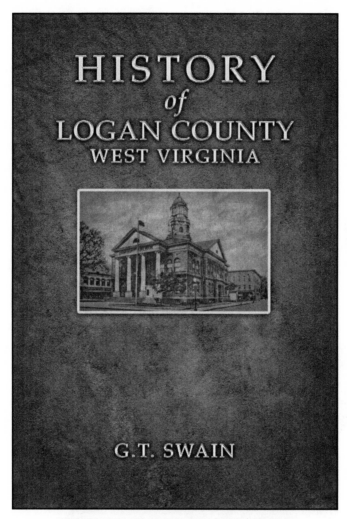

HISTORY OF LOGAN COUNTY, WEST VIRGINIA

Softcover. 384 Pages.

Originally penned in 1927, this book represents the history of Logan County, West Virginia. Includes the story of the settling of the region, the Hatfields & McCoys, Princess Aracoma, Blair Mountain War and the mine wars, and more.

THE FEUDING HATFIELDS & McCOYS

Softcover. 192 Pages.

In this volume, you'll find a timeline of events that tracks the history of the Hatfield migration westward in broad strokes, and tells the rich American story of the Hatfield & McCoy feud. This national bestseller was used as source material in the HISTORY channel documentary, *America's Greatest Feud: Hatfields & McCoys*. It includes many feud-era photographs and family stories that have been passed down through the children of Anderson "Devil Anse" Hatfield.

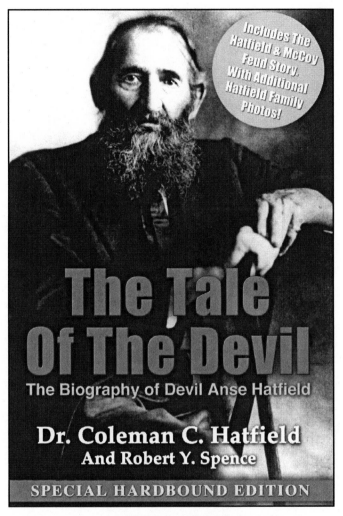

Includes The Hatfield & McCoy Feud Story, With Additional Hatfield Family Photos!

The Tale Of The Devil

The Biography of Devil Anse Hatfield

Dr. Coleman C. Hatfield
And Robert Y. Spence

SPECIAL HARDBOUND EDITION

THE TALE OF THE DEVIL

Hardbound Keepsake Edition. 330 Pages.

Now own a piece of the feud. This keepsake hardbound edition was used as source material in the recent HISTORY channel documentary, *America's Greatest Feud: Hatfields & McCoys*, directed by Mark Cowen and narrated by Kevin Costner. This book represents the first biography of Anderson "Devil Anse" Hatfield, meticously researched and penned by the Devil's great-grandson, Dr. Coleman C. Hatfield, and Robert Y. Spence. A national bestseller.

THE DEVIL'S SON

Softcover. 352 Pages.

The Hatfields & McCoys. You think you know who they were, why they fought, why they died. You know only the legend—now experience the real feud. *The Devil's Son* is a vast historical epic that breathes life into the individuals and families on either side of the Tug River. At the center of this novel is Cap Hatfield, second son of Devil Anse, the seminal figure in the feud. While the battle rages, Cap wrestles with coming of age in the shadow of the Devil.

Woodland Press, LLC

APPALACHIAN AUTHORS. APPALACHIAN STORIES.
APPALACHIAN PRIDE

Books Published In The USA
In Beautiful West Virginia

ATTENTION
RESELLERS / BOOKSTORES:
Stock Woodland Press Titles
By Contacting

Woodland Press, LLC

118 Woodland Drive, Suite 1101
CHAPMANVILLE, WV 25508

Bookstores, Writing Groups, and Retailers: If you would like to carry our catalog of book titles, or schedule a Woodland Press author to appear at your book event, contact us at email:
woodlandpressllc@mac.com

OR CALL
(304) 752-7152
FAX (304) 752-9002

www.woodlandpress.com

www.woodlandpress.com

CPSIA information can be obtained at www.ICGtesting.com
Printed in the USA
BVOW02s0802260813

329287BV00003BA/23/P